Kathy MAI

DANIEL O'DONNELL
My Pictures & Places

BOOKS

THE OFFICIAL ILLUSTRATED BOOK
DANIEL O'DONNELL WITH MICHAEL J McDONAGH AND EDDIE ROWLEY

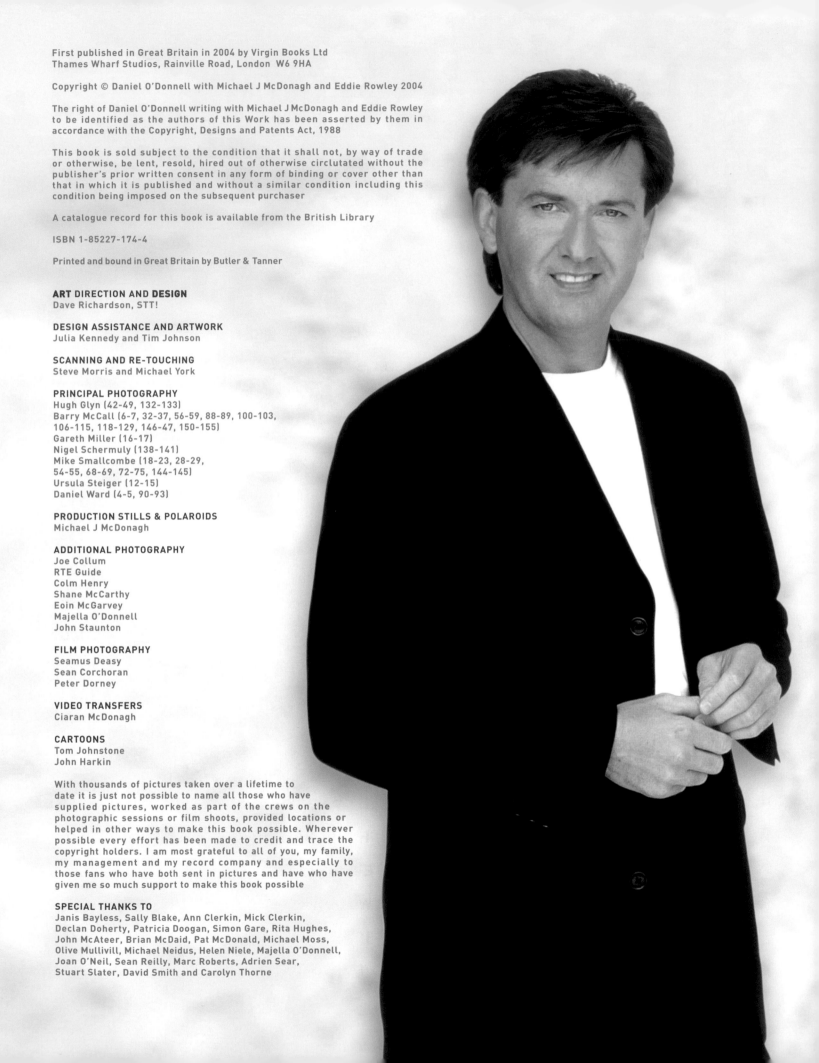

First published in Great Britain in 2004 by Virgin Books Ltd
Thames Wharf Studios, Rainville Road, London W6 9HA

A catalogue record for this book is available from the British Library

ISBN 1-85227-174-4

Printed and bound in Great Britain by Butler & Tanner

ART DIRECTION AND **DESIGN**
Dave Richardson, STT!

DESIGN ASSISTANCE AND ARTWORK
Julia Kennedy and Tim Johnson

SCANNING AND RE-TOUCHING
Steve Morris and Michael York

PRINCIPAL PHOTOGRAPHY
Hugh Glyn (42-49, 132-133)
Barry McCall (6-7, 32-37, 56-59, 88-89, 100-103,
106-115, 118-129, 146-47, 150-155)
Gareth Miller (16-17)
Nigel Schermuly (138-141)
Mike Smallcombe (18-23, 28-29,
54-55, 68-69, 72-75, 144-145)
Ursula Steiger (12-15)
Daniel Ward (4-5, 90-93)

PRODUCTION STILLS & POLAROIDS
Michael J McDonagh

ADDITIONAL PHOTOGRAPHY
Joe Collum
RTE Guide
Colm Henry
Shane McCarthy
Eoin McGarvey
Majella O'Donnell
John Staunton

FILM PHOTOGRAPHY
Seamus Deasy
Sean Corchoran
Peter Dorney

VIDEO TRANSFERS
Ciaran McDonagh

CARTOONS
Tom Johnstone
John Harkin

With thousands of pictures taken over a lifetime to date it is just not possible to name all those who have supplied pictures, worked as part of the crews on the photographic sessions or film shoots, provided locations or helped in other ways to make this book possible. Wherever possible every effort has been made to credit and trace the copyright holders. I am most grateful to all of you, my family, my management and my record company and especially to those fans who have both sent in pictures and have who have given me so much support to make this book possible

SPECIAL THANKS TO
Janis Bayless, Sally Blake, Ann Clerkin, Mick Clerkin, Declan Doherty, Patricia Doogan, Simon Gare, Rita Hughes, John McAteer, Brian McDaid, Pat McDonald, Michael Moss, Olive Mullivill, Michael Neidus, Helen Niele, Majella O'Donnell, Joan O'Neil, Sean Reilly, Marc Roberts, Adrien Sear, Stuart Slater, David Smith and Carolyn Thorne

CONTENTS

So many people make me feel so lucky. I have had opportunities and experiences that are not possible for some, but I have been able to gather so many happy memories and have made so many friends.

This book is a selection of those wonderful memories - especially for you. Thankyou for allowing me to follow my dream.

Love Daniel xx

ABOUT THE BOOK

Like every top singer and entertainer in the world, Daniel O'Donnell has had to grapple with modelling and acting roles in photo shoots for album covers and videos for his songs. Today, after a career spanning twenty years, those pictures and recordings, and the anecdotes surrounding them, give a fascinating behind-the-scenes insight into Daniel's world, the people he has encountered and the many interesting places he has visited around the globe. They also

introduce the reader to some of Ireland's beauty spots, which Daniel hopes will provide food for thought for your next holiday destination.

One man who was with Daniel every step of the way for most of his journey in pictures and on video is Mick McDonagh, the creative consultant who devised the first images of the young Irish entertainer. Mick continued to work with Daniel as the star went on to captivate audiences from Dublin's Gaiety Theatre to London's Royal Albert Hall, the Sydney Opera House to New York's Carnegie Hall. In *My Pictures and Places*, Daniel, in association with his co-writer Eddie Rowley, recounts his days with Mick in pictures and words, revealing some of their hilarious moments on the big photo and video shoots.

1. At the Coach House in Ballinteer with my brother James after a charity concert (late 80's)   2. Back row: my nephew John Francis, brother-in-law John, niece Patricia, me, my sister-in-law Brigid, brother John (Bosco), nephew Frankie; front row: my sister Kathleen, my mother Julia holding my nephew Daniel, sister Margaret (Margo), niece Fiona, nephew Joey   3. Taken in 1973 in Margaret & Bill O'Donnell's house on my holidays in New Jersey   4. With my nephew Daniel   5. Brian D'Arcy, Mother, me and Margaret (Margo) – taken during the Daniel O'Donnell shows on RTE in 1989   6. With my mother   7. Left to right: Kathleen (my sister), James (my brother), Margaret (Margo) (my sister), my mother Julia, John Bosco (my brother) and myself   8. My brother James, me in my sister Margaret's arms and Kathleen my sister   9. My nephew John Francis, sister Kathleen, my mother Julia, niece Fiona, nephew Daniel and niece Patricia at a fan club gathering in Dublin in 1991   10. Francis O'Donnell and Julia O'Donnell shortly after they were married   11. In my First Holy Communion suit

FAMILY BOY

As I sift through my old family photographs today, they spark off so many memories. I am lucky to be able to say that I had a happy childhood. So the recollections are good. Whenever interviewers say to me, 'You came from a poor background', it's not what I recall from that simple time in my life. By today's standards it was certainly poor. But I wasn't conscious of it at the time because everyone around us was in the same boat. There were only a few families who were better off. They were different. We weren't.

We always thought that the doctor and the teachers were a cut above the rest of us. Children and adults were on first-name terms, but doctors, teachers and their spouses were addressed more formally because of their positions in the community. The doctor's wife was always referred to as 'Mrs The Doctor'. The wife of a teacher called Jim O'Donnell (no relation), who lived in the village, was called 'Mrs Jim'. Being the youngest of the O'Donnell clan, I probably had a better lifestyle than my older siblings, John, Margaret (Margo), Kathleen and James. As I was the last, there was nobody seeking attention after me. I was home alone with my mother, Julia, from the age of ten, since everyone had left to pursue his or her own life by that stage.

My father had died when I was aged six. I don't think his passing caused me the trauma that the rest of my siblings suffered. I was very young and my father had spent most of his life working away from home in Scotland. I remember more about the death of my grandmother, since I was nine years old when that happened.

My mother has meant everything to me throughout my life. As a widow, left with young children, she had the sole responsibility for our upbringing. It was obviously a struggle for her. I'm glad that her twilight years have been good ones and that she has been able to share in my success. It was my mother who always encouraged me to sing and to enter local talent competitions. She'd say, 'Go up there and sing!'

1. My maternal grand parents James and Margaret McGonagle with one of their grandchildren   2. My maternal great grand parents Julia and Jimmy McGonagle   3. Last day at school with (top left) Noreen Walker, me, Geraldine Bonnar, Gloria McCole (RIP), (bottom left) Martina O'Donnell, Evelyn Ward, Breda Boyle   4. Left to right: James, Kathleen and me   5. Me with my sister Kathleen on my First Holy Communion day   6. My sister Kathleen and her husband John's baby Daniel on his christening day. Left to right: James, John Francis, John, Kathleen, me, Julia, Patricia and Fiona   7. Brother James, Marie Sharkey, me and Eugene Sweeney on my First Holy Communion day   8. Bib given to me by Jane Vilbrant on my first visit to Chicago in 1990   9. Annie McGarvey and me with Annie's old camera   10. Mum at home, 1999

10

I didn't mind, I enjoyed it. Later, when I left college to become a full-time singer, there was no opposition from her. Our mother let us all follow our own paths.

I don't recall knowing a time when my sister Margaret wasn't a successful singing star in Ireland. Her stage name was Margo. When I was seven, Margaret performed on Ireland's television chat show, *The Late Late Show*. Such was the prestige of that event that crowds turned out to greet her when she returned home. You'd think she had won the World Cup. Margaret was very young when she started singing semi-professionally. I remember her going off with the band in a van, taking her school homework with her! She will be forty years in show business this year (2004) and she's only fifty-three. Apparently, I used to say to Margaret that I would never become a singer. 'I could never do that!' I'd say. She often reminds me of that comment today.

Little did I know then that I'd caught the bug! When I followed my dream and became a singer, I had no idea that there were so many other sides to it. The fact that I would have to play the role of a model doing big photo shoots for album covers, tour brochures and publicity never crossed my mind. But I soon learned that it went with my life as an entertainer. Later, there would be big Hollywood-style productions for videos. It was beyond anything that I had imagined. I got used to doing picture sessions as the years went by, but I never grew to like them. To me, the big photo productions are a necessary evil. But at least I now have a great pictorial record of my career going back to 1985.

MY FIRST
PHOTO
SESSION

Daniel O'Donnell

The man who set up and directed my very first studio shoot is a guy called Mick McDonagh. Mick was working as a creative consultant to London-based Ritz Records, the company that launched my career. I would go on to work with Mick for many years in all kinds of interesting locations.

Recalling his first impression of me, aged 24, Mick says, 'The first time I saw Daniel he was singing at the Thatch on London's Holloway Road in 1985. I was convinced there was something very special about him. He had real star quality. He personified the boy next door at the time and that's the image I wanted to achieve on that first picture session. Daniel communicated with his fans so well on stage and it was my job to make sure that his pictures brought out his true personality.'

'I do think the first album cover *Two Sides Of Daniel O'Donnell* (1985) featuring Daniel in a yuppie suit, which now looks normal and tame but was very cool and so different for an Irish country singer in the eighties, made him stand out from the rest. It set the trend for our future work together as Daniel naturally developed his own unique style. We've had a lot of fun along the way and I am proud and privileged to be involved with him.'

That day Mick picked me up in his car at my friend Joan's house in London's Finsbury Park, and I remember feeling nervous about the experience that lay ahead of me as we negotiated the morning traffic. I had performed all over England, including London, by then, but I was on my way to a top photographic studio, and that was incredible to me at the time. Even though it was a professional job, it wasn't as elaborate as some of the later ones.

A friend, Ann O'Connor, had cut my hair for those first pictures. I brought some of my own clothes, including a suit, a pair of khaki trousers and a short-sleeved white top, with string netting on the chest and sleeves. I thought that top was the biz. It was very different from anything I had before. I felt I was heading in a very trendy direction. I wore that top until it became discoloured and I was sad to lose it, since I hated the thought of it going anywhere but with me.

Mick had employed a photographer called Ursula Steiger, thinking I would feel less intimidated working with a woman. But I couldn't relax. It didn't help that Ursula spoke English with what sounded to me like a German accent. It made her requests seem like commands. 'You will smile. You must smile,' she would say. Smile? I thought. I want to cry!

That was also the first time I was introduced to makeup for pictures. Ursula applied it and I cringed with embarrassment. It was also the start of Mick's obsession with flowers in my pictures and videos. I remember a tall vase with a single flower being used, which I didn't pay much attention to at the time. But in the years that followed Mick would be forever sticking a rose in my hand or flowers in the background during shoots. I used to think it was ridiculous. I think he only did it to torment me. I felt so inadequate during that first shoot. I didn't know how to stand or pose. Some say I look broody in many of the shots, but I wouldn't have known what broody was if it slapped me in the face.

One of the things I learned that day is that thirty shots might be taken just to get one picture. I couldn't understand it at the time. Why so many pictures in one suit? I now know that it could be the slightest wee thing that sparkles and that's the best picture. That's where Mick's talent was invaluable to me.

I NEED YOU

After the trauma of my first photo shoot, my next big ordeal was making a pop video for a song called 'I Need You'. Once again, Mick was at the helm, creating the scenes. Lights! Camera! Action! I wondered where it had all gone wrong for me. I was a singer. If I'd wanted to become an actor I would have gone to Hollywood, I thought. It soon became painfully obvious that I was no actor. I was as awkward as a ballerina in clogs. To add to my discomfort, there was a love scene. I wanted the ground to open and swallow me up.

The video was shot at a couple of locations around Dublin, near Donnybrook and outside No.5 Herbert Park on the south side of the city, as well as in the Grafton Street area. In one scene I'm lost in love, peering out of the window of a house on a leafy road. Then I head off on my bike, wearing a grey coat with a red scarf. I'm sure the shoppers around the city's South Anne Street/Wicklow Street were wondering who I was. Not many would have known me then.

Eventually I meet the girl who has captured my heart. She was a lovely blonde young woman called Debbie Bowes who had been hired for the video. Mick hadn't met her until that day, because she had been cast by a record company, and he felt she was far too glamorous for me. The cheek of him! The makeup department apparently toned her down! In the video we have a romantic dinner and I pop the question at the end of the evening. I remember getting the ring out and trying to smile as I clumsily put it on her finger.

Then the dreadful moment arrived when I had to do my first – and last – screen kiss. I was afraid to be too enthusiastic about the kiss, in case she might think I was doing it for real. That's how naïve I was! I was tremendously shy and was glad when it was all over.

The next evening I picked up the Irish *Evening Herald* and spotted my video fiancée modelling underwear! God only knows what she thought of me.

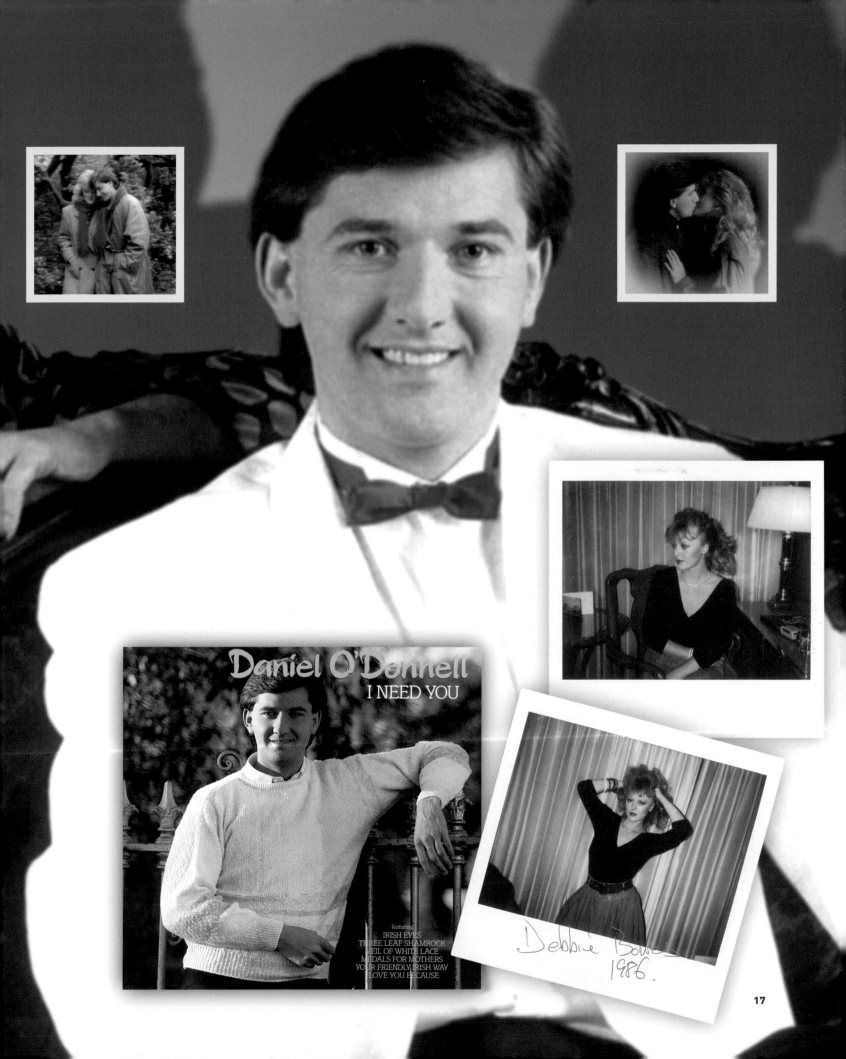

Daniel O'Donnell
I NEED YOU

featuring
IRISH EYES
THREE LEAF SHAMROCK
VEIL OF WHITE LACE
MEDALS FOR MOTHERS
YOUR FRIENDLY IRISH WAY
I LOVE YOU BECAUSE

Debbie Bowes
1986.

Looking back, if there was one positive feature of the many dreaded photo shoots that seemed to come around faster than a flash of lightning, it was the opening of doors to a fashion world I might otherwise have never investigated. But I can also say, without fear of contradiction, that, whatever image people have of me today, it's one that is totally home-grown. I am one hundred per cent organic. No artificial fertilisers were used! Contrary to what any of the critics might think, I am not the product of some style guru. Nobody ever got a chisel and carved out this performer Daniel O'Donnell. People may have bought me clothes for photo shoots and TV shows, but nobody ever tried to mould me. Whatever way I am today is because of how I developed naturally.

SESSION

time out shopping for clothes for a shoot and we were looking at outfits I wouldn't have thought about. It was an exciting experience. One of the items was a black polo-neck sweater and I really took a shine to it. At first I wasn't too sure about it, but when I tried it on with a shiny, cotton summer suit it looked really well. The next day I went to America and I took the suit and polo-neck with me. I liked them that much! There was also a yellow rugby shirt and jeans.

The one feature of my appearance that I'm very fussy about is my hair. It pays not to let too many people mess with it because I still have it, you see. I'm also lucky to have retained my natural colour without having to resort to the bottle. I threw caution to the wind on that second shoot and let their hairstylist called Simon Bryer have a go at my crowning glory. What a relief when I looked in the mirror afterwards. My hair was styled, ruffled and textured. I was delighted with the combination of the new hairstyle and the sharp clothes and professional makeup. It was the biggest makeover I'd ever had, although the difference was mostly the haircut. I haven't altered that much since then.

That photo session took place in a big house and it was all very surreal to me. I thought it was amazing to be involved in such a major production and it was all for me! I was obviously enjoying the process a bit more. But that was also the first time I realised my hair was receding, so there's a downside to everything. Thankfully the tide hasn't gone out too far since 1988, as there's still plenty of it up front.

Passing through Dublin Airport on my way home from England one day, I was surprised to see a massive billboard advertising my album, FROM THE HEART. The photo session for that album in 1988 produced a picture that was my favourite from that period. I was wearing an olive-green sweater and the photo was taken against a deep-green backdrop. I loved the colour scheme and the 'look', because I felt it captured how I like to see myself.

It was that same photo staring back at me as I skipped through the airport that day. Then I noticed a feature in it that hadn't been obvious to me before. There was a line of dust on the back of the chair I was sitting on. It was there to be seen by every visitor to Ireland. When I mentioned it to Mick the look on his face was priceless. He hadn't spotted the flaw either. His mind had obviously been on flowers the day the photo was taken at a studio session in London.

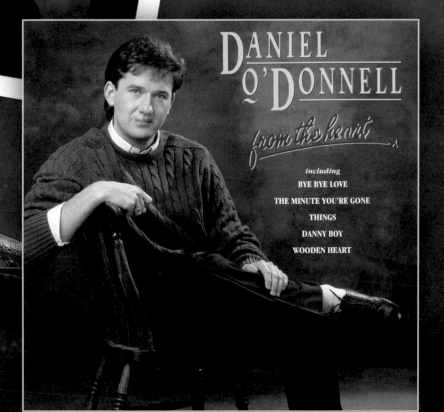

The old wooden chair had been lying around the studio and Mick thought it would look good in the picture. He wiped the dust off it, but missed the back. We had a good laugh over it. I like to think the dust added a little extra character to the photo. And maybe it shows that I'm not perfect after all!

DANIEL O'DONNELL

from the heart

including

BYE BYE LOVE

THE MINUTE YOU'RE GONE

THINGS

DANNY BOY

WOODEN HEART

American country legend Loretta Lynn and Britain's Cliff Richard are my idols, but there's another singer who has also inspired me and that's the wonderful Vera Lynn, the woman who became known as the forces' sweetheart during World War Two. Vera Lynn was born in London in March 1917, and she's had a remarkable career. By the age of seven, she was singing on a regular basis in working men's clubs. Up to the age of fifteen, she performed in a dancing troupe.

However, it was during the war that Vera found fame. In 1940, she started her own BBC radio show called *Sincerely Yours*. During the programme, she would read out messages from loved ones to their soldier boyfriends, husbands and sons. She became their link with the men fighting abroad. With hit songs such as 'We'll Meet Again' and 'White Cliffs of Dover', Vera was catapulted into what is now referred to as superstardom.

She also made three films, *We'll Meet Again*, *Rhythm Serenade* and *One Exciting Night*, and she travelled abroad to entertain the troops, becoming Britain's most popular female entertainer. In fact, Vera became the first British singer to get to Number 1 in the American charts with her single, 'Auf Wiedersehen, Sweetheart'. A woman called Joan Tobin, with whom I stayed in England, was a fan of Vera Lynn and she knew that I admired her greatly.

In 1989, Vera was due to give a performance at London's Festival Hall and, to my surprise, Joan got us two tickets. Well, I really looked forward to that concert with the excitement of a child in the countdown to Christmas. I had never, ever seen Vera perform live on stage. It was going to be a real treat. Imagine then how I felt when Mick called to say he had lined up a photo shoot for the *Thoughts of Home* long form video and album cover on the very day of Vera Lynn's concert. 'No problem, Mick,' I muttered, not at all pleased. But, I thought, at least we can do it early in the day and I'll still make the show in the Festival Hall. Then Mick dropped the bombshell. The shoot was at the Aghadoe Heights Hotel near Killarney in Co. Kerry, Ireland. I won't repeat what went through my mind.

Album cover shot. (isle of Innisfree).
2nd of frame. (commercial slid)

Album cover / commercial
begin frame.

"Take me to
Vera Lynn"

"Where the long
light shakes across
the lakes"

LORD TENNYSON

Well, on the day of the shoot I was like a hen on a hot griddle. I was anxious and checking my watch every five minutes. Mick eventually noticed that I was on tenterhooks.

'What's wrong, Daniel?' he asked.

'I'll tell you what's wrong, Mick,' I replied. 'Vera Lynn's performing in London tonight and I'm going to be in that audience by hook or by crook.'

I could see by the look on Mick's face that he wasn't too optimistic about my chances. Then fate intervened. There was a horse in the field where we were doing the photographs and he galloped over to us, kicking over cameras and causing enough damage to force the cancellation of the shoot. There were horrified faces all around me. I was delighted. I'm allergic to horses, but I could have kissed that one! Fair play to Mick, he got me a seat on the next flight out of Kerry.

There was a party of nuns on the plane and I think one had been left behind to let me on. That sister will get her reward in heaven, since I got to see Vera Lynn sing that night, after a mad dash to the theatre. I even sneaked backstage and shook hands with her, and it's not like me to do that. I had got so carried away with the thrill of her performance. Vera was 74 at the time, but she was still magnificent.

Before the horse did me a favour, they had taken pictures of me in a yellow sweater. But they had planned to feature me in a blue one as well. It was decided that blue suited the cover, so they later got an expert to hand-paint the yellow one!

My friend the horse!

FUJI-RDP

John 'Riverdance' McColgan.
August 29. 1989.

Signing the record contract with Neil Palmer (Telstar) and Mick Clerkin (Ritz Records) 1989

C O N C E R T

They say it's an ill wind that doesn't blow some good. In 1992 I was forced to stop singing and performing, due to a combination of problems with my throat, as well as physical exhaustion. It was my body's way of telling me that I was doing too much work. That period was a very worrying time for me and I didn't dare contemplate the prospect that it was the end of my days on the stage, a place that was heaven on earth to me. Through conventional medicine, natural healers and faith healers – I wasn't leaving anything to chance! – I slowly recovered and returned to the limelight after a break of four months. But that health scare changed the way I would work from then on.

After that, I made the huge leap from playing at dances to becoming exclusively a concert performer. My very first large-scale concert, after my return to the stage in 1992, was at the Point Theatre in Dublin. The Point had not been on my radar up to then. To me, it was the natural home to big pop and rock concerts and massive stars. If it had been left to me, I'd never have done it. It was a huge gamble at the time. I wasn't at all confident that I could attract enough people to fill the venue, which can hold six thousand seated. My health hadn't yet been fully restored, but I'd felt well enough to go back. My manager Sean Reilly and the Irish concert promoter Kieran Cavanagh worked tirelessly to make it a success.

Such was the excitement they generated around the event that it was a full house on the night. I didn't want to leave the stage, the atmosphere was so good. Up to then, I had done concerts in the UK, but, apart from a week at Dublin's Gaiety Theatre in 1987, I hadn't cracked the Irish concert scene. As a result of illness, I had made the giant leap and it brought me to another level.

Now I do a concert tour in Ireland every year and it's very successful. From the moment I first stepped out on stage at the Ragg – a venue in Thurles, Co. Tipperary, back in January 1981 – I had been singing at dances. There's hardly a dance hall or pub in Ireland that I didn't perform in. But eventually my voice suffered from the smoke and the dust from the dancing, and I would get hoarse. I have fond memories of performing concerts at the Gaiety Theatre and I've always loved London's Royal Albert Hall. I love the atmosphere in it. It's a wonderful venue.

There's no venue in which I would find it intimidating to perform nowadays, but I remember the fear that gripped me when I first performed in the Dominion Theatre on London's Tottenham Court Road. I was playing support to Brendan Shine (an Irish entertainer). Standing in the wings, I realised that the stage was bigger than some of the entire venues I was playing at that time. I looked at the microphone sitting in the centre of it, and the distance from where I was standing seemed like miles. I'll never know how my legs carried me to the mike stand that night.

29

Sometimes I don't look my best in live pictures, because when I'm singing there's no time to pose...

HI DANIEL, IT'S MÁIRE RUA AGAIN!

30

DANIEL
O'DONNELL

CREW

BROCKWELL LIMITED   PASS NO.

6   THE SUN, Thursday, August 4, 1994

DRESSING
ROOM

STAGE

Tom Johnston

"RIGHT, LADS ... HERE COME THE GROUPIES!"

31

There is nowhere in the world I feel more complete than in my homeland of Donegal. It's the nearest place to heaven on earth for me. I have been fortunate to get the opportunity to travel and to visit many countries and locations throughout my life as a singer. I've seen breathtaking beauty and wondrous sights of nature on my journeys. But, still, no matter what those destinations had to offer, nothing compared to Donegal. That's where I feel totally at home and nothing will entice me away from it. Even if I spent only one month of the year in Donegal, I would still refer to it as home.

It's more than the place: it's the people; it's where I grew up; it's the place that helped to shape me into the person I am today; it holds all the memories from my childhood. Today, when I drive around the area and spot the different landmarks, I'm reminded of another time in my life. There's the Cope, a general store that takes me right back to the age of nine when I started working part-time in it. That was a great growing experience for me as a person because of the interaction I had with the people of the community. It developed my personality, helped my confidence to grow, and subconsciously I was picking up the skills of dealing with the public, which was obviously an advantage later in life.

The Cope was the village store and it stocked everything from animal feed to wellington boots. At first, I was given menial tasks such as sweeping the floor; then I graduated to weighing the corn, layers' mash, chick mash and corn cake for the cows. The Cope also had a delivery van and, eventually, I was sent out on that as a helper. That was significant because it was the first time that I became known to people around

D O N E G A L

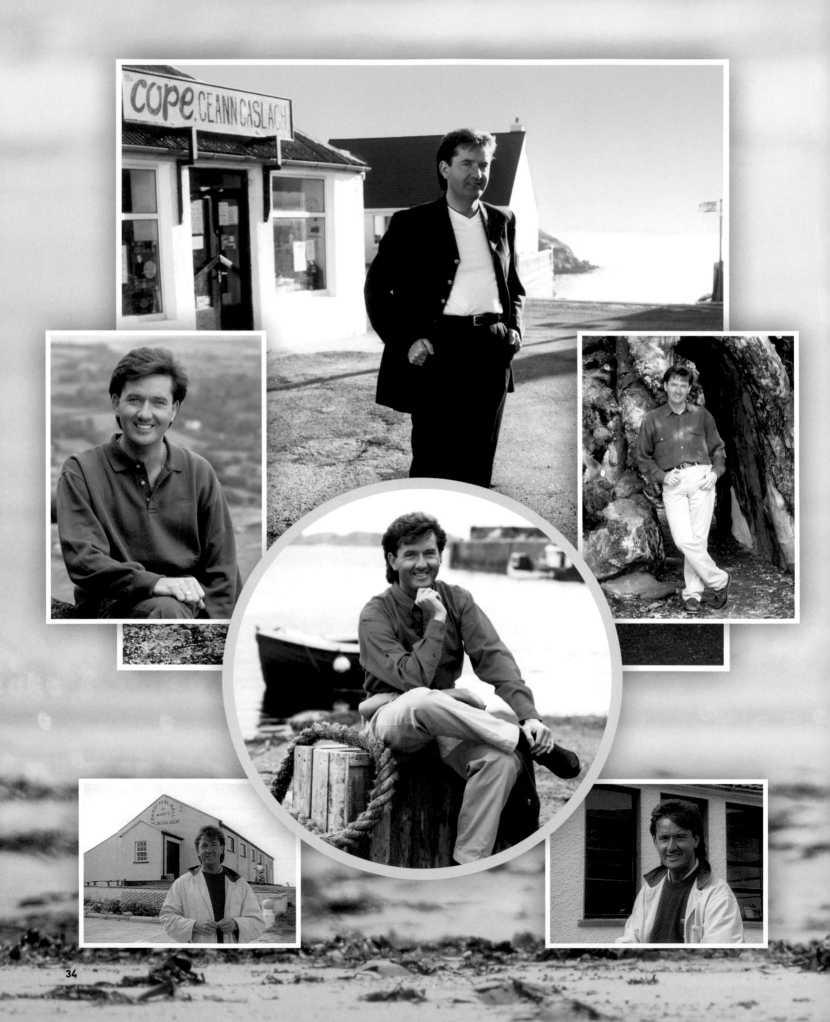

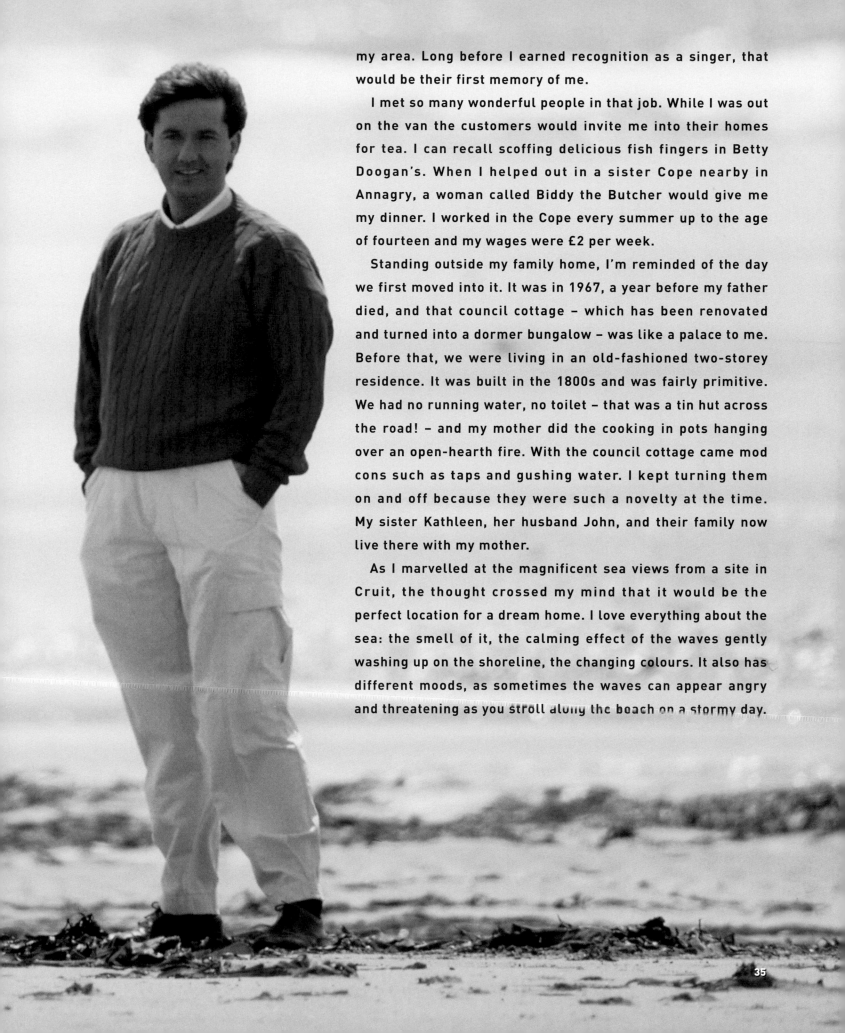

my area. Long before I earned recognition as a singer, that would be their first memory of me.

I met so many wonderful people in that job. While I was out on the van the customers would invite me into their homes for tea. I can recall scoffing delicious fish fingers in Betty Doogan's. When I helped out in a sister Cope nearby in Annagry, a woman called Biddy the Butcher would give me my dinner. I worked in the Cope every summer up to the age of fourteen and my wages were £2 per week.

Standing outside my family home, I'm reminded of the day we first moved into it. It was in 1967, a year before my father died, and that council cottage – which has been renovated and turned into a dormer bungalow – was like a palace to me. Before that, we were living in an old-fashioned two-storey residence. It was built in the 1800s and was fairly primitive. We had no running water, no toilet – that was a tin hut across the road! – and my mother did the cooking in pots hanging over an open-hearth fire. With the council cottage came mod cons such as taps and gushing water. I kept turning them on and off because they were such a novelty at the time. My sister Kathleen, her husband John, and their family now live there with my mother.

As I marvelled at the magnificent sea views from a site in Cruit, the thought crossed my mind that it would be the perfect location for a dream home. I love everything about the sea: the smell of it, the calming effect of the waves gently washing up on the shoreline, the changing colours. It also has different moods, as sometimes the waves can appear angry and threatening as you stroll along the beach on a stormy day.

I find the sea a very relaxing place to be around. You can lose all sense of time and reality and get lost in your own thoughts. Little did I think that day in Cruit – as I admired the view and thought what a nice place it would be to live – how fate would smile on me and I would later realise the fantasy.

Everywhere I go on tour today I invite people to come and visit Donegal, which, incidentally, stands for 'fort of the foreigner'. It's so-called from having fought off numerous Viking raids in the eighth and ninth centuries. These days, all are welcome! I am confident that each and every visitor will be touched by the magic of it. And Donegal really is a magical place. You could drive for just three miles and see one hundred different views. The landscape is constantly changing with every turn of the road.

Much of the county remains sparsely populated. Its thousands of acres of moors, mountains and lakes ensure that Donegal remains one of the last true wildernesses left in Europe. Along the 650 kilometres of coastline, which has been shaped over thousands of years by the relentless actions of the mighty Atlantic Ocean, there are many sheltered bays and Blue Flag beaches for the tourist to enjoy in the summertime. Overlooking much of this coastline are rugged mountains and hills. It's been said that in Donegal you can experience rain and sunshine at the same time, and the climate is very changeable due to the influence of the Atlantic Ocean. But this all adds to the appeal of the place. I have yet to meet anyone who hasn't enjoyed their visit.

When people talk about their trip to Donegal their two main comments usually concern the friendliness of the people and the beauty of the landscape. If you're reading this and have never had the experience of a holiday in my native county, don't go to the grave without having had that pleasure. Once visited, it remains in your heart for ever.

GUESS WHAT?
IT'S RAINING AGAIN!!

Singing in the rain has never been my idea of fun. I hate the rain and I don't like being in it. But when you're working in the great outdoors of Ireland it goes with the territory. Mick and his team would make plans for video and photo shoots and God would smile. Over twenty years, I've spent a lot of time on the stage, but I've also passed more time than I care to remember sitting under an umbrella with the rain spitting down all around me. The expressions on my face certainly don't hide my feelings about that experience!

There is no better backdrop for photographs and videos than the beauty spots of Ireland, which are truly spectacular. But if you could transfer the climate of somewhere like Tenerife to my country, even just for the photo shoots, I would be a very happy man. There is no joy in sitting under an umbrella in the cold and the wet. I shiver as I recall days of rain when we've been shooting in places like County Leitrim.

My enthusiasm for photo shoots has a very short life span at the best of times. I quickly grow very tired of smiling for the camera. And when the rain comes it certainly doesn't lift my spirits. I start getting frustrated then, and Mick would be no help. I'd get twice as irritated watching him running around hanging flowers on the trees, as if nature weren't able to do its own job! Whatever fixation he has with flowers, it doesn't make any sense to me.

It's amazing to think how a few drops from the sky can upset such a big production. Mick would be desperately trying to prevent them falling on my shirts. I might be wearing a blue shirt or some light-coloured top, and if drops got on them all the crew would be flapping

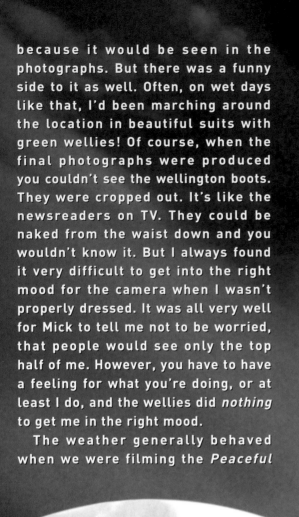

because it would be seen in the photographs. But there was a funny side to it as well. Often, on wet days like that, I'd been marching around the location in beautiful suits with green wellies! Of course, when the final photographs were produced you couldn't see the wellington boots. They were cropped out. It's like the newsreaders on TV. They could be naked from the waist down and you wouldn't know it. But I always found it very difficult to get into the right mood for the camera when I wasn't properly dressed. It was all very well for Mick to tell me not to be worried, that people would see only the top half of me. However, you have to have a feeling for what you're doing, or at least I do, and the wellies did *nothing* to get me in the right mood.

The weather generally behaved when we were filming the *Peaceful*

Mick, waiting to be discovered, are we?!

Daniel

40

Waters video on the boat, unlike Mick, who was sticking a rosebush on the stone wall of an old church during the shooting. Perhaps he ought to have been doing a television gardening programme. But the day we were doing the photograph for the video cover, it was lashing out of the heavens, with the wind kicking up a storm. The great advantage of being the star of the show is that you have to stay dry, but the rest of the crew got soaked to the skin trying to get the perfect shot that day. Of course, as God knows, there's no pleasing people. On good days the photographers complain that it's too sunny and too bright!

Thurs July 15, 1993

My video for 'Old Fashioned Love' was a real Hollywood affair – it even had a helicopter shooting scenes from the sky! I took a step back and reflected on how it was a long way from my early days on the road with a band, as I struggled to become established as a singer.

Back then, we were travelling the length and breadth of Ireland and the UK in vans that often broke down in the middle of the night, leaving us stranded. A helicopter was never part of the dream in those days! One of the main locations for 'Old Fashioned Love' was my home at Rathcoole outside Dublin, where I was living at the time. Mick was directing operations from the sky – movie mogul Steven Spielberg had some serious competition way back then! – and he discovered that they couldn't land at my house because of a big power pylon. Mick then put a mobile call into my near neighbour, the Irish comedian Brendan Grace, seeking permission to land on his lawn. Brendan, being an entertainer, was still in bed and Mick woke him up. Naturally, he was a bit grumpy on the phone.

'I can't hear you,' he roared. 'There's some madman in a helicopter flying around my house.' Mick and the cameraman, Seamus Deasy, eventually landed safely in Brendan's garden and the hilarious comic appeared in his bathrobe, looking like Henry VIII and waving his fist. The pylon was a good excuse. At least the flowers in my garden were still there after the helicopter, while Brendan's were now in the near-by town of Naas!

Speaking of flowers, Mick was up to his old tricks again and he shoved a rose in my hand as I was filmed around the shops of Naas in full view of the locals. I felt like a right prat. One of the highlights of the video is some old footage from Mick's sister's wedding in Manchester from 1960, but he hadn't told her. She married a TV producer and it was on the local news, but she'd never actually seen it. By a strange quirk of fate she was watching Country Music TV in New York when 'Old Fashioned Love' came on. Imagine her shock when she spotted herself as a bride thirty years previously!

Old Fashioned Love – Altrincham, Aug 4, 1960

ONED LOVE

DANIEL O'DONNELL

What Ever Happened To Old Fashioned Love

3-TRACK COMPACT DISC SINGLE

Brendan Grace

Fashion Designer, Pat, Toronto, 33 years later!

JUST

FOR

YOU

44

DANIEL O'DONNELL

AN INTIMATE MUSICAL

1992 was a very eventful year in my life, both career-wise and on a personal level. It was the year that I suffered serious health problems and was forced to go off the road. It was the year that I became a concert performer after making a triumphant return to the stage four months later, with people travelling from all over Ireland, the UK and even Australia for the show in Dublin's Point Theatre. It was the year that my native county of Donegal won the All Ireland Football Championship for the first time ever in the history of the sport. And it was the year that I made my very first appearance on *Top of the Pops*.

Just For You is a behind-the-scenes documentary video that was made around that busy time in my life and, among the highlights, was a tour of my native Kincasslagh to show people where I grew up. While in Dublin, I was filmed singing the popular ballad 'Dublin in the Rare Auld Times' and then we went up to Blessington, a scenic area of Co. Wicklow, where I sang 'Singing the Blues' and 'The Old Rugged Cross'. The song that really stands out from that period is 'I Just Want To Dance With You'.

When I was recording my *Follow Your Dream* album in 1992, that was the last song I did in the studio. The Irish singer Mary Black had recorded it and I took a shine to it. At the time it was a little different from what I was doing. It was heading more towards pop. But I went into the studio and I said, 'I would really like to record this song.' Once I recorded it I knew there was something different about it. I remember playing it for a couple of people and one person in particular, who wouldn't have had any interest in my music, was really impressed. 'You should make a single out of that,' he said.

I hadn't thought about releasing 'I Just Want To Dance With You' as a single, but Mick Clerkin of Ritz Records and my manager, Sean Reilly, saw its potential. So we made a single out of it and Sean and I went off on a promotional trip to Australia. While we were there, Sean got the news from home that the single was doing

exceptionally well in the UK pop charts and it might go into the Top 40. It actually went up to Number 30 and then we heard there was a chance I might get the opportunity to do *Top of the Pops*.

I couldn't believe it. Like every teenager, I had been a fan of *Top of the Pops*. I remember watching Suzi Quatro, David Essex, Gilbert O'Sullivan, Elton John and Cliff Richard on it, never thinking that one day I might be there myself. I left Australia a day early with the hope that it was going to happen. Sean phoned home on the stopover in Singapore and it was confirmed. I could have flown the rest of the journey without a plane!

I went shopping myself for my *Top of the Pops* outfit. I wore a short jacket because they were 'in' at the time. I thought I looked like a million dollars that day. But, despite the 'cool' gear, I still felt out of place when I arrived at the TV studios and was mixing with all the trendy young pop acts of the day. Still, they

Wicklow '94

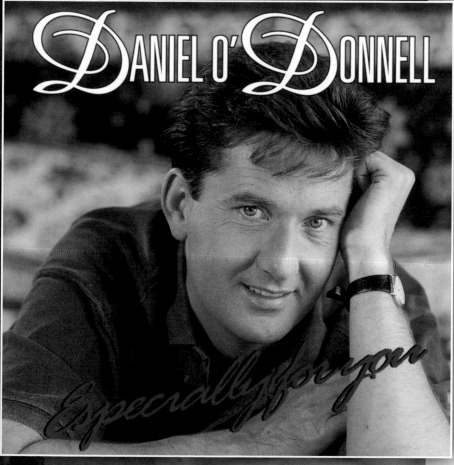

were all very nice to me and I savoured the experience of performing on that show. It was a really big deal to me and to everyone back home in Kincasslagh.

The following Sunday I joined the rest of the people from my native Donegal as we marched on Dublin's famous Gaelic games stadium, Croke Park, to see our team bid for our first All Ireland senior football victory. We were up against the Dublin footballers and their supporters didn't give us a chance. 'Show the boys from the hills what it's like to be in the big city,' some of them were shouting behind me during the match. Another said there'd be white blackbirds flying the day we won the Sam Maguire (the All Ireland football cup).

Well, I don't know about the white blackbirds flying that day, but 'the boys from the hills' showed the Dubs what it's like to be in the city with the Sam Maguire in your possession after we beat them! On the way home in the car I turned on the radio to listen to the UK Top 40 countdown. 'I Just Want To Dance With You' had jumped ten places to Number 20. It was like a double victory for Donegal, since that was a major achievement for me at the time. Life couldn't have been sweeter at that moment. It seemed that the gods were on my side.

Speaking of the supernatural, we had a very funny incident during the recording of the *Just For You* documentary in Blessington. It was decided that I should be filmed singing 'The Old Rugged Cross' in a local graveyard with a suitable cross in the background. The shooting ran late that day, so it was dark by the time we got around to it. A generator was set up with a long cable to focus a light on the rugged cross and, out of respect for the location, I recorded the song with the sound quite low. Earlier that evening we had noticed that visitors had set up quite a large camp site on the other side of the wall, but by morning they had mysteriously disappeared. Apparently they had scarpered after being terrified of the cross glowing in the dark, and the strains of music coming over the wall!

Over the twenty-odd years that I've been performing, my shows, albums and videos have branched out to include songs of faith and inspiration. They have given new depth to what I do and I have found them to be personally uplifting and fulfilling. Judging by the response from the people who follow my music, they have touched the hearts and souls of many other people too. There was such a positive reaction to the recordings that it seemed only natural that I should build a live show around those wonderful songs.

In 1997 I did my first gospel show at Dublin's Point Theatre and because it was such an amazing experience we decided that from then on it would become a regular extension of what I do. That show developed from an album called *Songs of Inspiration* and it featured favourites such as 'I Saw the Light', 'One Day at a Time', 'My Forever Friend', 'You'll Never Walk Alone', 'What a Friend We Have in Jesus', 'How Great Thou Art', 'Amazing Grace' and 'Standing Room Only'. As I listened to the *Songs of Inspiration* album I thought, Wouldn't it be wonderful to do a show combining gospel and Christmas music?

In my regular tour I didn't get the opportunity to feature either of those selections in its entirety. That night a new show was born and it's a performance I personally look forward to every year. I have performed it in venues such as London's Wembley Arena and the National Exhibition Centre in Birmingham.

In August 2003 I had the incredible experience of doing a Songs of Faith video in front of an audience at the Mahony Hall in Dublin's Helix Theatre, accompanied by my band, the 60-voice Irish Philharmonic Choir and a 63-piece orchestra, along with the Omega Singers and my touring partner Mary Duff. We did 37 songs during the two hours. The show was recorded and it is available on video and DVD.

I was in heaven for that couple of hours. There may have been an army of us on the stage, but we all connected to make it a very moving and energising affair. I especially enjoyed my duets with Mary Duff on the gospel/country classic 'Will the Circle Be Unbroken' and the universally loved standard, 'He's Got the Whole World (In His Hands)'. The choir were particularly strong on 'I Watch the Sunrise' and 'When Darkness Falls', while the Omega Singers did a rousing version of 'Rivers of Babylon'.

I am blessed that my career has incorporated that style of music and that the people who enjoyed my regular shows have also joined me on that journey. At Christmas time it's always a great thrill for me to combine the gospel music with carols and traditional songs of the festive season. It's a lovely way to bring the curtain down on my year.

When I look back over my career, I can see several big highlights. There have been numerous great moments. My singing has taken me along so many different paths. I'm glad that my mind and my heart have always been open to new directions for me as a performer. It may seem strange that I can do an inspirational album one year, followed by a rock'n'roll collection. They used to say that rock'n'roll was Satan's music. I don't think so. I think God might have been a rocker and, sure, didn't Jesus have long hair!

★ THE OMEGA SINGERS ★

THE GOSPEL SHOW
FROM THE POINT

TV SHOWS

After all these years, I still don't take a television appearance for granted. I feel it's a great achievement to get on the box. After all, there is now so much variety out there in show business. The pop industry, in particular, has so many artists vying for the big entertainment and chat shows. It's nice to know that there is still a place for Daniel.

I feel very comfortable in a TV studio these days, whether it's in Ireland, the UK, Australia, New Zealand, Canada or the States, but I was a bundle of nerves at the start of my career in the eighties. I would be fretting about it for weeks beforehand and getting over it for weeks afterwards.

Around the time of my album, *I Need You*, back in 1986, there was a very popular afternoon Irish TV show called *Live At Three*, and I was invited on. That was tremendously exciting for me because I felt I was moving up the ladder when I was getting recognition on national TV for the first time. I can still remember what I wore: grey trousers with a light-grey sweater.

When I first started performing with my band in small Irish venues, I could never have foreseen an honour like *This Is Your Life* down the line. I was performing as a guest on Bruce Forsyth's variety show from the London Palladium in 2000 when Michael Aspel presented me with the famous red book. When I spotted him arriving out on stage I thought he was heading for another guest, Engelbert Humperdinck. My jaw hit the ground when he said, 'Tonight, Daniel O'Donnell, this is your life!' It was an amazing honour and a well-kept secret by my management, band, family and friends.

I love doing *The Late Late Show* in Ireland because it's an institution. I grew up watching it when Gay Byrne was the presenter. When you appeared on *The Late Late Show* you were certain that everyone in the country was going to see you because it was so popular. Gay has now retired, but the show itself lives on with a new host, Pat Kenny, who has also been very supportive of me. Another famous Irish-born TV personality, Terry Wogan, also had me on his show, *Wogan*, in the UK and that was special at the time.

There have been stand-out moments for me in TV through the years. *Songs of Praise* in the UK became a very important show for me and I even presented one of them. It was actually my first TV exposure in the UK back in the late eighties. Harry Secombe was the presenter and I sang 'The Old Rugged Cross' just below Errigal Mountain in Dunlewey, Co. Donegal.

Appearing on *Top of the Pops* was a lovely surprise in 1992 and I'll never forget the honour of doing a big millennium show in Cardiff, singing 'Light a Candle', the theme song for the show. Cliff Richard was on that spectacular, too, and no matter what I'm on with Cliff I enjoy it because I really admire him.

My career has gone off in a new direction in recent years with America opening up for me. That has been due to the Public Broadcasting Service (PBS) TV network across the States. They are now supporting me, playing my recorded shows and having me on as a live guest. As a result of PBS, I now have a big following in North America. To achieve that at this stage of my career has been both surprising and thrilling. But that's the power of television!

1. Michael Aspel, This Is Your Life   2. Top Of The Pops   3. Marty Whelan and Mary Kennedy, RTE
Open House   4. Sir Harry Secombe, Songs Of Praise   5. Maxi, RTE Radio 1 DJ   6. Gloria Hunniford,
Open House   7. Gay Byrne, The Late Late Show   8. PBS Television, USA

I'm not the type of person who pays much heed to horoscopes. They say a fool FOLLOWS the stars and a wise man RULES them. I'm a Sagittarian. Without researching what that says about me, I will tell you how I see myself. My characteristics, in my view, are that I'm a calm person with determination. I've read that a Sagittarian is direct, frank, open, impulsive, outspoken, jovial, affectionate, enterprising, active, self-confident and quick of comprehension, and loves the freedom of outdoor life and travel. There's plenty to choose from there! According to the experts – and who am I to argue with them? – I'm probably the most delightful and charming companion that you will find.

Apparently, Sagittarians are not only out to enjoy life, but are imaginative and fun-loving. One of their best traits is a good sense of humour. Always filled with new ideas and enthusiastic about each of them, those of the sign of the archer are ambitious and generous. Sagittarians, it is said, will enjoy almost anything anywhere, so they are easy company. You shouldn't have any trouble striking up a conversation with them, since they have a variety of interests.

I like this one: 'The Sagittarian is intellectually stimulating and fascinating to talk with.' Sagittarians, for the most part, say what they feel, regardless of how it may sound, although they wouldn't hurt anyone on purpose. So how does all of that apply to me? Well that's for other people to judge.

When I was a child growing up in Kincasslagh, the local town of Dungloe was a major outing for me, even though it was only six miles from where I lived! There was only one return journey on the bus, so you'd have to stay for the day before catching a ride home.

The world has got a lot smaller since those simple times. I still find it quite incredible that I can now visit the UK, Australia, New Zealand, America and Tenerife — all in the one year! That really is jet-setting. But most people from all walks of life now travel to foreign parts on annual holidays. There are more flights nowadays and air travel has become cheaper. It has opened up all kinds of wonderful experiences for all of us.

I love getting away to the sun, and Tenerife is my favourite because it's familiar to me and I think I like familiarity. I like that sense of knowing the surroundings, and the fact that my wife Majella's parents are there is an incentive to visit. Tenerife, of course,

NIAGARA FALLS
MEMORIAL ARENA
NIAGARA FALLS CANUCKS
NOV 1 VS PORT COLB 730
NOV 22 23 CHARLEY PRIDE
NOV 23 24 DANIEL O'DONNELL

Skiing with Majella

JENNIFER
AMERICANA
THEATRE

EURO COUNTRY
MUSIC MASTERS '8

will always have a special place in my heart, because it was there on holiday that I met Majella for the first time.

When I started going to Florida I thought, Wouldn't it be lovely to spend more time here? Majella and I then started looking for a holiday home and we found one that was just perfect. We really fell in love with it. It was only when we started living there that we discovered that we had jumped in without doing our research, which was silly of us. The problem was, there was no nightlife and I think Irish people can't survive without nightlife. We cannot survive without the pub culture and I'm someone who doesn't even drink! But I love a singsong and having the craic (fun), and there was none of that in Florida, so we sold up.

I like going to warm places, so I like touring the likes of Australia. I like the feel of the warmth on my body, but I've gone off sunbathing ever since I started spending a lot of time in the sun. There's no point in helping nature to speed up the ageing process, and I don't want my face to wrinkle up like a prune!

F R I E N D S

There isn't a day goes by that I don't give thanks to God for all the blessings I've enjoyed since I've been successful as a singer. It's true to say that I've lived a charmed life. It's been very rich, and I'm not talking in terms of money or material things. I'm referring to the opportunities it has given me to cross paths with so many people I've admired. They say you should never meet your idols because the general opinion is that you'll be disappointed by them. I must be lucky, then, because mine have lived up to my expectations and more.

If I didn't have this life and had found a magic lantern, I would have asked the genie to grant me two wishes. To meet the American country singer Loretta Lynn and Cliff Richard. I'm so lucky to be able to say that both of those have been granted. In fact, beyond all my dreams, they have both been to my home village of Kincasslagh. And I am privileged to state that I can now call them personal friends.

Loretta Lynn, in my book, shines above every other entertainer in the world. I love her singing and I love her as a person. She is my all-time favourite singer. As fans know, for many years at my local Donegal Shore Festival of Kincasslagh there has been a surprise 'belle of the ball' organised for me. In 1997, I nearly fainted when I turned around and saw that it was my own living legend, Loretta, in the flesh.

I've met Loretta on many occasions and the thrill has never diminished. When I walk up to her she knows me and I can't adequately tell you how much that means to me. If I can make one person feel the same about me, then what I do is worthwhile.

Since I've been married I've no longer needed a belle, so in 2003 the organisers of the Kincasslagh festival came up with the idea of a surprise guest for me. When the strains of 'Living Doll' filled the air I was gobsmacked. It was Cliff. Since I got to know Cliff, I've been able to confirm my opinion that he's a real gem. He's a genuinely nice person.

Charley Pride is another gentleman of country music that I've had the honour of getting to know. Majella and myself have met Charley and his wife Rozene socially and they're two very hospitable and easy people to be around. When I met Dolly Parton I could see why she wowed the world: she has such a great personality. Another great lady of country was the late Tammy Wynette, whom I met at Wembley in London back in 1988. Before Garth Brooks became a superstar I got to know him briefly while I was recording in Nashville. He had just gone on the road for the first time and he was talking about the buzz he got from it.

While doing TV shows I often bump into other guests, and I met Bono from U2 on *The Late Late Show* in Ireland. I really admire how he uses his celebrity status to campaign against injustice in the world and he has been a great ambassador for our country.

The day I got my MBE, I met Prince Charles for the first time and I loved his dry sense of humour. I wouldn't mind spending time with him. I think Charles is very entertaining and I suspect he has some great one-liners. I've also had the honour of getting to know the Irish president, Mary McAleese, and singing for her at Aras an Uachtaráin, the presidential home in Dublin's Phoenix Park. We had tea on the lawn and I offered her one of my buns. That's the kind of laid-back atmosphere she generates around her.

Sometimes I feel guilty that I'm able to meet those people without any effort. As I have said already, it's a charmed life, but I do appreciate it.

& HEROES

1. Receiving MBE from HRH Prince Charles   2. Close friend Josephine Burke & Irish soccer star Packie Bonner   3. Martine McCutcheon & Sally Blake   4. The Judds   5. Lesley Garrett & Eamon Holmes   6. U2's Bono & Marc Roberts   7. Pat Kenny & Majella   8. Tom Johnson cartoon for The Sun   9. Loretta Lynn   10. Gerry Kelly   Main Picture, with Cliff Richard

1. Irish tenor, Finbar Wright   2. Cliff Richard   3. Coronation Street lads   4. Dolly Parton and Gloria Hunniford   5. Westlife   6. Sandy Kelly
7. Garth Brooks   8. Philomena Begley   9. Crystal Gayle   10. Charley Pride   11. Susan McCann   12. Eastenders cast   13. George Hamilton IV
14. Four Tops   15. Michelle Collins   16. Rolf Harris

You should always be careful of the invitations you extend to people. Little did I know when I invited fans to drop by for tea to my family cottage in Kincasslagh that five thousand would one day turn up! I'm sure my sister, Kathleen, said a few 'prayers' for me that day, since she was entrusted with the role of offering a cup of tea to each and every one of those visitors. I have to admit that I never expected so many people would come. And they queued, patiently, for hours along the rural hill leading down to the house. It was a sight to behold.

My annual tea party was born out of the international 'Mary From Dungloe' festival, which has been running in our area since 1968. It's our 'Miss World', attracting crowds of fifty thousand or more to the county of Donegal during the week-long festivities. People come from all over Ireland, the UK and as far away as New Zealand, Australia and North America for the big event, since I always mentioned it on my tours abroad.

During their trip, many of the fans went searching for my home and some even called in to say hello. More often than not, I would be out and they would go away disappointed. I find it difficult to talk to a lot of people on a day when I'm singing. So I then decided to designate a date and a time when I would definitely be present to meet one and all, and I announced it at my shows. Call me naïve, but I honestly didn't realise that so many people would take me up on the offer.

At first there were hundreds and over the years thousands started arriving. It became such a phenomenon that the media began picking up on it. One day I looked out to see TV crews from Ireland, as well as the likes of Sky News, and even NBC from America, covering the event. My main concern, then,

Kathleen made over 1,200 cups of tea!

was how such a massive influx of people would affect my neighbours in Kincasslagh. I wondered whether I had created something that should not have been imposed on such a small community. But, to their credit, the local people rose to the occasion and made everyone feel so welcome, and that, too, filled me with a sense of pride. It was a great period in my life and what gave me real satisfaction was the fact that it brought people together and friendships were formed along the roadside during the hours that the fans queued.

I would love to be thought of as somebody who brought people together. All good things come to an end at some stage, and we eventually had to bring the curtain down on the open day. Really and truly it became a victim of its popularity. It got to a point where there were just too many people to cope with. Towards the end I felt I was only getting the chance to see a fraction of the crowd. I feared that the fans were ultimately going to be disappointed with the experience. But it was a great time in my life and the wonderful memories remain with me.

They say the camera never lies, but photographs of me working out in a gym are a long way from the reality of my life. To me, a gym has the same attraction as a torture chamber. I have no great desire to end up in either of them. But for this particular photo session the weather conspired to have a gymnasium as a backdrop to some of the shots.

This shoot was due to feature the sights of London in the background, but when morning arrived I pulled back the bedroom curtains to see a menacing black sky and a thunderstorm brewing. Wild horses weren't going to drag me outdoors that day. It was decided to set the session in an apartment at Charterhouse Square, not far from where we were staying in London. It was owned by Dave Richardson, who designed my CD covers.

The apartment was in the building that is used as the home of *Poirot*, of the BAFTA-award-winning TV series featuring Agatha Christie's famous Belgian detective. There was a gym in the basement, so photographs were taken there. I was flexing muscles I didn't have! There was a swimming pool and I was pictured there in a white towelling robe. And later, during a break in the awful weather, I donned a white T-shirt for some outdoor shots in the square. Looking at them you would think it was a lovely spring day.

FLORIN COURT

INTERIOR POIROT COURT

Florin Ct Gym

MY TEAM

I once had a lovely letter from a fan who is wheelchair-bound. In it, she said that when I look at her I see a person in a chair, rather than a chair with a person in it. That sentiment reminded me so much of my manager Sean Reilly. He sees the human element in me, not just the product that I provide. Without a shadow of doubt, Sean is the best person that I could have met career-wise. There is nobody in my career that I hold in higher regard. We have a great relationship and a great friendship. We travel the world and we never have a disagreement. We are similar types of people. We have the same general formula for life. It's been the perfect marriage.

It was Mick Clerkin of Ritz Records who introduced me to Sean at the beginning of 1986. I was in the process of joining Mick's record company at the time. Mick told me that Sean was a manager with many years' experience in the business. My first manager was a lovely lady called Nan Moy, but Nan and I both realised that we were never going to make it together. We parted company as friends and we're still friends today. Mick Clerkin was the man I needed in my career at that point. He had seen me perform at a festival in 1985 and recognised that I had potential. I was looking for a way forward and I was thrilled to see his interest in me.

Mick advised me at that time to stop what I was doing, take a break and come back in a different way, with a new band. It worked. I am for ever grateful to Mick and everyone at Ritz Records. I think I must be a lucky person because I've attracted great people in my life. What I have achieved wouldn't have been possible without a team effort. You cannot build an empire on your own.

Without my band, of course, there wouldn't be a show. The current line-up features Ronnie Kennedy, who has been with me since 1985. Billy Burgoyne, Tony Murray and John Staunton joined me in 1986. John Ryan and Kevin Sheeran were in my band from 1988 until 1992 when I took the break. When another band member, Richard Nelson, left in 2002, Kevin rejoined me. John is still my producer in the recording studio. Raymond McLouglin has been with me since 1992 and Stephen Milne came into the show through Mary Duff's band. He has been with me since 1996.

There is also a great support crew working behind the scenes to make the shows happen. I appreciate the fact that they are the real stars too. Without guys like Joe Dunne, Paddy Doyle and Glyn Owen, who drive, set up all the equipment and make sure everything is in perfect working order, I could not function. Padraig Grogan has been doing the sound since the late eighties. John Brown is the man responsible for the lighting and Gary Warner does the monitor sound, which is the sound I hear on stage. The quality of the sound is obviously a very important feature of my live shows and Pat and Alan Nolan Amplification are the people who have supplied our equipment throughout my career.

People who come to my shows will also have seen Robert Kennedy and my niece Patricia Doogan on the merchandising stand. Backstage there's a very important lady called Loretta, who is my personal organiser. Loretta looks after all the mail that I receive at the theatres. Before shows I sit down in the dressing room and try to answer as many letters as possible.

If Britney Spears can have a 'minder', well so can I. Joe Collum needs no introduction to the fans. He's like my shadow. Joe has become a very close personal friend. I'd be lost without him. I would say he's a great ambassador for me because he has a great way with people. He can be firm, but in the nicest possible way.

Both Sean Reilly and myself would have chaos in our lives if it wasn't for the support of a very important lady called Joan O'Neill. Joan is Sean's personal assistant and our tour manager.

I am also very grateful to Ann Clerkin and all the staff in the London office, May Lynch and the team in our Dublin headquarters and everyone in our organisation who makes it possible for me to do what I do as a singer.

1. Sean Reilly 2. Mick Clerkin 3. The Band 4. The Whole Crew
5. Ann Clerkin 6. Joe Collum 7. Loretta Terry 8. May Lynch
9. Joan O'Neil 10. Nan Moy 11. John Ryan 12. Eddie Rowley
(Sunday World) 13. Patricia Doogan 14. Robert Kennedy

Like many people in the world of entertainment, I've chased the American Dream. To achieve a good level of success in the States is a little bit special. I tried it early in my career, but it was a really daunting challenge.

America is so vast. You could be a big star in one state, but nobody would know you in the one next door. To make an impact would have involved relentless touring there, and I didn't have the luxury of time on my side to devote to it. It would have meant moving to the US for a long period and turning my back on the people who were following me at home and in the UK, Australia and New Zealand. It was too much of a gamble. That's not to say I didn't dip my foot in the water. In 1989 I went to Nashville to record my country album, *The Last Waltz*. I was working with their local producer Allen Reynolds, who has turned out international hits for artists such as Garth Brooks, Don Williams and Crystal Gayle.

I was a little apprehensive going into the studio, as I wondered what Allen and the local musicians would think of an Irish guy singing country songs. But my fears were unfounded, as I felt very valued by Allen and all the people I met there. With the benefit of hindsight, I now realise that there was

Daniel O'DONNELL

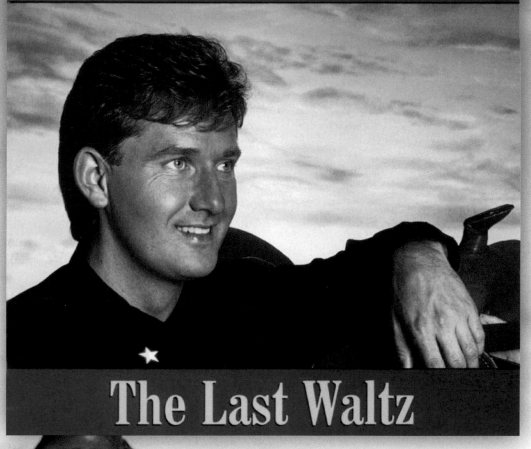

The Last Waltz

no need for me to record *The Last Waltz* in Nashville. The thinking behind it at the time was that if I had an American producer and American musicians the album would be more acceptable to the people in the business in America. But it made no difference at all. Allen said at the time that if I lived there for a year I would probably do very well, but I didn't want to move to the US. Now, after twenty years in the business, America is happening for me thanks to the support of the PBS television network there.

Incidentally, we didn't do the photo shoot for *The Last Waltz* in America, but in a studio in London. Mick created the background by introducing a Western saddle and painting a pink sunset sky. Did you notice the silver star on my black shirt? That was another of Mick's bright ideas, cut out from a piece of kitchen foil. No expense spared!

As I drove up a sweeping path past lovely estate cottages and a picture-postcard old church in the English countryside of Leicestershire, the thoughts going through my mind reflected on the interesting world my singing had opened up to me. I was on my way to a new adventure, doing a photo shoot at an old country house hotel. I was excited about it because I had never explored this part of the countryside before.

As our car reached the end of the long driveway the first glimpse of Stapleford Park was an impressive experience. I felt like royalty at the prospect of staying there. Stapleford is a very elegant country house hotel, both inside and out. Its history spans over a thousand years, and it only became a hotel in 1986. I learned that Queen Victoria's son, Edward, Prince of Wales, liked it so much that he wanted to purchase it. His mother prevented him from doing so in case, it is said, his morals might be corrupted by the Leicestershire hunting establishment. They bought Sandringham instead, which is just as well because otherwise I wouldn't have had the opportunity to stay at Stapleford or get a feel for what it's like to live in such a grand place, as well as being photographed in the beautiful surroundings.

FORD PARK

Inside, the lobby had a roaring fire and there were stuffed heads of animals on the walls. Each of the 51 rooms had been styled by a different designer, ranging from Liberty to Pirelli. All of them had views over the park and were kitted out to the last detail.

I was allocated one of the main suites and I felt very special indeed. It had a warm, relaxing atmosphere and was sheer luxury. I picked the right job in life, I thought. There was work to be done, of course, and the rooms were perfect locations for photographs. Lots of shots were taken of me relaxing in the plush surroundings and dining in the olde-worlde restaurant. Mick also persuaded me to have a picture taken in the bath, but, before you get too excited over that affair, I'll have you know that I was wearing swimming togs to protect my modesty! I got my own back on him later when I encouraged Traolach, the hairstylist, aided and abetted by the rest of the crew, to chop off Mick's shoulder-length silver locks. The devil can be in me sometimes!

We liked Stapleford Park so much that we returned there on another occasion to shoot a TV commercial and video for 'You Needed Me' outside the ancient St Mary Magdalene church in the grounds. Stapleford is still a very popular place to stay.

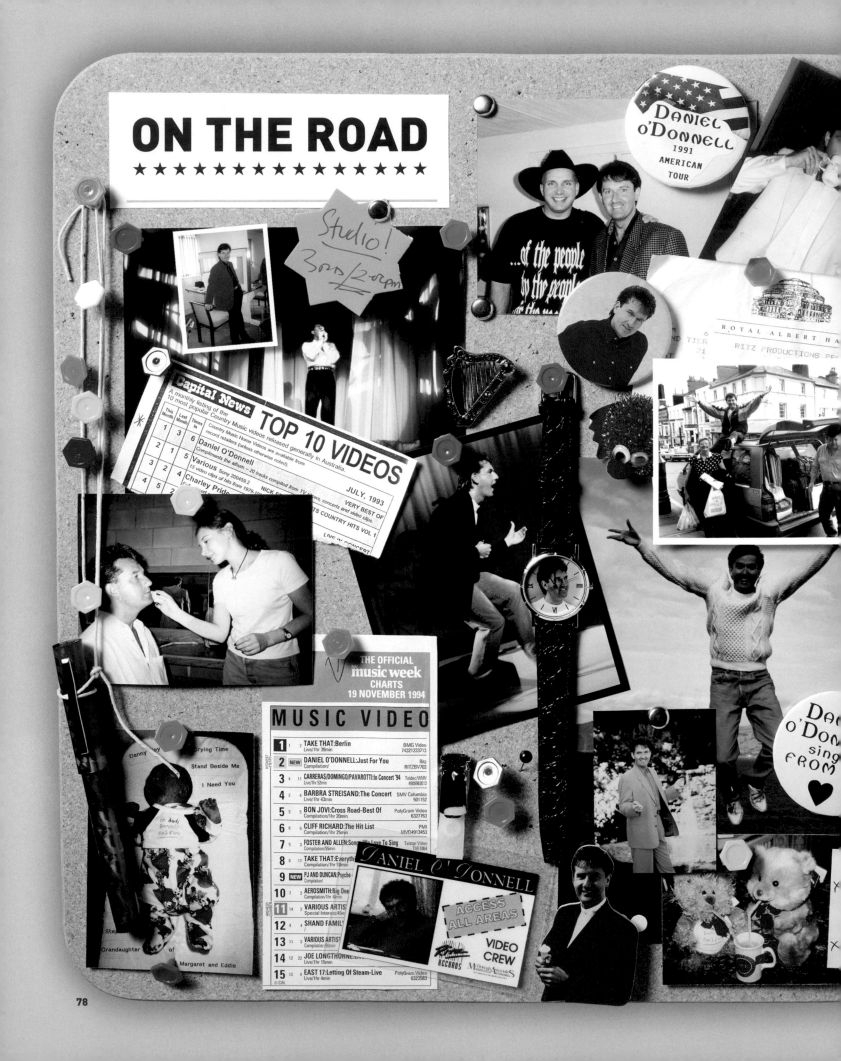

ON THE ROAD

★★★★★★★★★★★★★★★★★★★

Studio!
3pm/2:00pm

DANIEL
o'DONNELL
1991
AMERICAN
TOUR

...of the people
by the people

ROYAL ALBERT HALL

RITZ PRODUCTIONS

Danny Boy   Crying Time

Stand Beside Me

I Need You

In dad's
Daniel's
has fun

Grandaughter of
Margaret and Eddie

DANIEL O'DONNELL

ACCESS
ALL AREAS

VIDEO
CREW

RECORDS

Da
o'Do
sing
FROM
♥

As jobs go, mine is a strange one. I'm constantly on the move, living out of a suitcase and sleeping in a different bed almost every night. That's the lifestyle of a touring singer. But it's no bother to me at all. I love every aspect of it and I never get bored. I've often heard entertainers complaining that it's a hard life. I've honestly never felt that it is, with the exception of the time I was overdoing it and ruining my health. To me a hard life would be working on a building site or farming. This is like my hobby.

Of course, there are degrees of touring. When you get a bit of success you can do it in comfort and today we travel well and stay in good hotels. It wasn't always like that. When I was struggling to launch a solo singing career, I was virtually broke. I remember being down in Dublin with so little cash that one day I had to decide between a Big Mac with chips in McDonald's and walking home, and just having chips, which would leave me with enough money left over for my bus fare home. I was so addicted to McDonald's at the time that I ended up walking home!

In the early days I'd often take turns driving the van with the band as we journeyed through the night up and down the motorways in the UK. Funds were so tight at the time that I remember how the entire band, including mo, had to share a room in a Travelodge one time because that's all we could afford. After my health scare in 1992, I changed my lifestyle on tour. I used to be doing things morning, noon and night. I'd do interviews, official openings, hospital visits, you name it, by day. I'd nearly turn up for the opening of an envelope. And then I'd do the show that night. Now, while it goes against my nature to say no, I just rest during the day. My total focus is on the show, because I have to protect my voice.

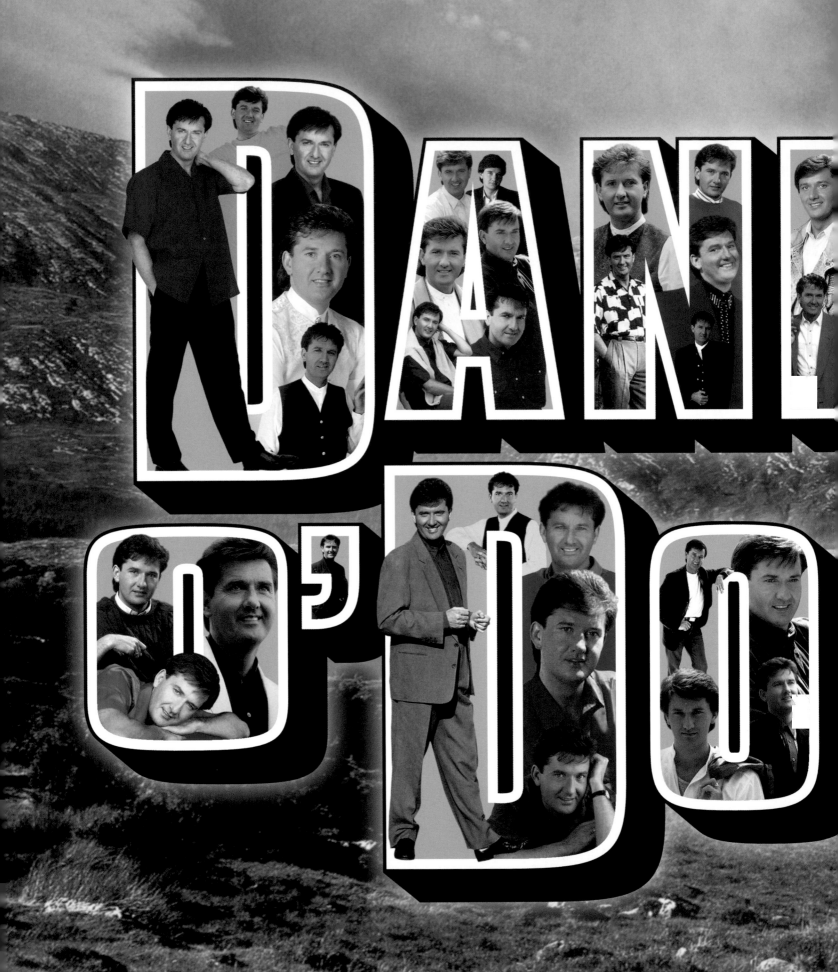

MY FRIENDS

I have the most wonderful relationship with the people who enjoy what I do as an entertainer. The term 'fans' is not one I'm comfortable using: I prefer to think of my audience as friends. And I enjoy meeting them away from the stage, which other people in show business find difficult to understand. It's not something I do to court success: I truly, honestly enjoy the interaction with each person. If the people who follow me get as much enjoyment out of our personal contact as I do, then it's worthwhile for all of us.

As a result of getting up close and personal with the people who are fans, I always see familiar faces when I look out at the audience during my concerts in Ireland, the UK, Australia, New Zealand and North America. I love that feeling of knowing people, it makes me feel very comfortable, and that probably comes from my background, growing up in a small rural community.

One great memory I have of being with 'the fans' was our first trip to Branson, Missouri, in 1997, when I was accompanied by people from all over Ireland and Britain. Eight flights took people out! Two of the fans, a couple called Marie Fallon and PJ Tierney from County Galway, Ireland, got married in Branson during the trip, with Mary Duff and me doing the honours of bridesmaid and best man, and everyone who had travelled over to see my shows filling the church to witness their special day!

The day I stop meeting fans will be the day I retire from performing. And I want to stop a week before I get to the stage when I'm not good enough to perform well. I think almost every entertainer goes on too long. I've told a lot of people to let me know when my day comes around.

Thank you to all my fans and friends around the world who have helped to make it all possible. I've tried to fit in as many memories of you as I could into these photo pages.

83

Joe 'David Bailey' Collum

The big, draughty old Dublin warehouse, with its cold walls and empty shell, could not have been less glamorous for our video and photo sessions to accompany the duets album, *Timeless*, which I'd recorded with my touring partner Mary Duff in 1995. Here I have to marvel at the creative skills of Mick and his ability to create something at very short notice. Within a couple of hours Mick and his crew had transformed the stark interior into a very impressive Ginger Rogers-style Hollywood film set. They worked like a team of ants and I was amazed at how, with a shortage of materials, they improvised.

It was like one of those TV makeovers. They hung swathes of cheap muslin from the ceiling, found some old plaster columns in a skip outside and painted the floor white. When the lights were set up the set looked really impressive. It had all the hallmarks of a very expensive production, but it cost next to nothing, as it was all junk from a skip enhanced by clever lighting. Mary and I then performed the song together using an old-fashioned microphone, with a gentle wind machine blowing in our faces. I have fond memories of that session and not just because it was all done in one morning.

Working with Mary is always such a pleasure as she's a real gem. I am very lucky to have Mary as part of my touring show, as I feel we really complement each other. The audiences really like her and I love the duets. I don't naturally sing harmony – it's like learning another song – so I just sing along with what Mary is singing. Nobody ever told us to sing duets – it was my suggestion.

I had thought of our doing the song 'Somewhere Between' together, and the first time we sang it was at the Ulster Hall in Belfast. It was such a big hit that the duets became a regular feature of my show. In addition to the title track, *Timeless* also includes 'We Believe In Happy Endings', 'I Won't Take Less Than Your Love', 'Whispering Hope', 'Have You Ever Been Lonely', 'I Heard the Bluebirds Sing', 'Eileen McManus', 'Secret Love', 'Vaya Con Dios', 'Walk Right Back', 'A Girl I Used to Know', 'Jeanie's Afraid of the Dark', 'Somewhere Between' and 'Will the Circle Be Unbroken'.

8/2/96

DANIEL O'DONNELL & MARY DUFF

Timeless

TCR 01:09:15:08

TCR 01:04:08:14

TCR 01:16:20:11

TCR 01:23:07:18

Early call!!
Thurs May 18th, 1995

As I swished back the curtains in my hotel room, the panoramic views that greeted me were startling. I was in Wales, having arrived from Australia under the cover of darkness in the middle of the night. But as my eyes scanned over the streets and buildings in the morning light, I could have been forgiven for thinking that I had landed in a little Italian village.

The year was 1995 and we had travelled to a place called Portmeirion to do a photo shoot for my album, *The Classic Collection*. Once again, I marvelled at how my singing had taken me to somewhere extraordinary – in this case an interesting and picturesque Italianate hillside village near Porthmadog in the north, a part of the world I might never have otherwise discovered.

This was a real gem with its fairytale streets, cottages and shops. Naturally, I was keen to explore the area and delve into its history to find out where the Italian influence had originated. But first, Mick insisted on taking some shots of me to capture my morning facial stubble.

Afterwards I did a little research on Portmeirion and soon learned that it was the work of an eccentric British architect called Clough Williams-Ellis. He owned the private peninsula, which is set on the scenic coast of Snowdonia in Wales. The reshaping of Portmeirion was Williams-Ellis's personal hobby and it kept him occupied for fifty years, starting in 1925. I'll stick to the golf myself! But, to his credit, Williams-Ellis did a marvellous job and it was obviously a labour of love.

You can see how much thought and painstaking work he put into the project. It could have all gone horribly wrong, but Williams-Ellis proved that you can develop a naturally beautiful site without destroying it. His lifelong concern was with architecture, landscape, design, the protection of rural Wales and conservation generally. I hear he travelled the world looking for all kinds

of odds and ends for this project. Like an antiques collector, he was constantly searching for colonnades, porticoes, gazebos and various assortments that would delight the eye of everyone who visited this quaint village on a wooded slope overlooking Tremadog Bay.

As I wandered in the early morning along the cobblestone streets up steps and through arches, I could see it was a really special haven of tranquillity and a place of beauty. That first morning I felt I wasn't in the real world at all. I had travelled to Wales, but stepped into a place that was of another country. The rooms and surroundings reminded me of the movie, *Under the Tuscan Sun*, the story of a just-divorced writer who buys a villa in Tuscany on a whim, hoping it will be the start of a change for the better in his life.

Portmeirion is now owned by a registered charity, the Second Portmeirion Foundation. All the cottages in the village are let as part of the Portmeirion Hotel and there are several shops and restaurants. It's surrounded by the Gwylit subtropical gardens and woodlands and miles of sandy beaches, and I would highly recommended it as somewhere special to visit. Portmeirion Hotel enjoyed a celebrated clientele from the start, including George Bernard Shaw, who was a regular resident. The village has also been used as a location for movies and TV dramas. In 1966 it was the setting for the cult television series *The Prisoner*, starring Patrick McGoohan. And *Brideshead Revisited*, the TV miniseries starring Jeremy Irons, Anthony Andrews, Laurence Olivier and Claire Bloom had some scenes filmed around the area.

As a backdrop for photographs, you really couldn't go wrong in Portmeirion and the whole crew were very pleased with the end product for my shoot. *The Classic Collection* features eighteen songs including 'The Minute You're Gone', 'A Little Piece of Heaven', 'Distant Drums', 'Little Cabin Home on the Hill', 'Old Photographs' and 'Moonlight and Roses'.

HAPPY
Christmas

Season's Greetings

DECEMBER
25
Christmas Day

Daniel O'Donnell

Christmas
with
Daniel

96

Wishing You A Very Happy & Peaceful Christmas

4. I saw Mama Kissing Santa Claus
Restaurant Int.

WHITE CHRISTMAS

12. C.H.R.I.S.T.M.A.S.
SCHOOL CLASSROOM INT.

97

Wishing you a merry Christmas.

Merry Christmas

10. SILVER BELLS
JEWELLERS, DUNGLOE   EXT.

An Old Christmas Card
Shed/Attic Int.

8. SANTA CLAUS IS COMING TO TOWN
BY XMAS TREE IN FRONT OF JEWELLER
EXT.

Christmas, as I have mentioned, often arrived in May and June for me. It was just like being in the movies. Every year I send out personalised Christmas cards and they have to be prepared months in advance, so I'd often find myself doing a Christmassy photograph in the early part of summer. In that way, unlike most, I got to experience Christmas twice a year!

One of the biggest video shoots I've done in Donegal was for my 'Christmas With Daniel' release in 1996. That was a spectacular affair. The locations were around my own Kincasslagh and the nearby town of Dungloe and that shoot caused quite a stir. Hollywood had arrived in Donegal.

There were some very funny reactions from people who weren't aware of what we were up to. We set up Christmas shop window displays at the Cope store, and toy shops, and a large civic Christmas tree was erected in Dungloe. Even though it was the end of May, the weather that summer wasn't very good, and we had to leave everything in place for a few days until the conditions for filming improved. This caused some passing tourists to stop and do a double take.

I believe there was a letter in the *Irish Times* from someone who had passed through the area and was wondering whether Dungloe was the earliest town to get its lights up for Christmas – or were the authorities just bone idle about taking them down from the one gone by? We shot a Christmas dinner scene in the home of a local friend, Paddy Forker's house at Cruit, next door to where I now live.

There was one very embarrassing incident in which I had to act out a scene doing Christmas shopping, just as all the locals were coming out of the pubs at closing time. I'm sure they thought, Who does he think he is, Pierce Brosnan? Mick insisted on doing one big scene in the local church, but the priest wasn't too happy about it. However, our Mick can be very persuasive and eventually he reached a compromise to get his way. The priest took the day off and handed over his church, provided that all of us involved in the filming be respectful, move little and stay not too long.

Well, God forgive us, as soon as the poor man's back was turned, Mick had the crew removing all the pews to get his moving cameras in on their tracks; and the team was in the church from 6 a.m. on the day until 2 a.m. the *following* day! There was a scene in the church where a dove was released while I was kneeling and singing 'Christmas Story' and 'The Gift' at the altar. That was a real disaster.

First of all, I'm no fan of birds. I'll let you in on a secret here: it's not that I dislike them, but I'm actually afraid of them. I don't like them to come close to me. There was worse to come. The bird obviously hadn't gone to acting classes because when it was released, instead of flying up in the air it dropped in front of me, looked uncomfortable, and laid an egg on the floor!

So Mick tried again. This time the bird flew towards the ceiling like a rocket and smashed off a rafter. Now at that point I understood why it wanted to escape, because it was freezing cold in the church, it was late at night after a long day, and my enthusiasm had long since worn off. But the bird eventually performed like a star on the third attempt. It obviously wanted to go home too!

We had a lovely children's choir performing in the church that day as well, but they nearly set fire to each other with the candles! Fortunately, no children, animals or birds were hurt in the production.

The experience of doing photo shoots and video recordings around Ireland down through the years introduced me to many of its natural beauty spots. I realised that we inhabit one of the most fascinating islands on the planet. You could spend a lifetime exploring its nooks and crannies and still not uncover all there is to see and appreciate.

And I think, as native people, we take it for granted and don't go out of our way to discover our own country. Instead, we prefer to go to foreign destinations for our holidays and adventures. Sometimes we go sightseeing only when we have visitors to be entertained. For my own part, I have to admit that, if it wasn't for my singing career, I might have missed many opportunities to enjoy the natural beauty on my doorstep. Mick was always trying to find locations off the beaten track around Ireland as a backdrop.

I loved the shoot we did in Donegal's Poison Glen at the foot of the majestic Errigal Mountain, which is the second highest in Ireland. This is the glen at the head of Dunlewey Loch and there are many theories about its strange name in English. The most popular opinion is that it's an incorrect translation of its name from Irish, which, in fact, means 'heavenly glen'. And that's exactly what it is. It's a magnificent place with absolutely breathtaking scenery. I was pictured at the entrance near the famous old Dunlewey roofless church, which looks forlorn standing alone beside the lake, but has a beauty of its own.

This was a Church of Ireland building erected by the landlord of Dunlewey in the 1830s for the small Protestant community that worked in and around the estate. I remember walking through fields and stepping on sheep droppings while

Cameraman Seamus Deasy and his assistant Fiona, focusing on the green wellies!

Away with the fairies...

On Castle Island

under Mick's direction, which gave him a great laugh. It was at this location I did the first *Songs of Praise* TV programme, which was presented by Harry Secombe.

There was also a funny little cottage, occupied by a woman who claimed that she was a white witch. When you went through the gate it was like going into another world. She wasn't crazy or anything like that, but she told me that there are fairies there and that she had built a turret for them. Do I believe in fairies? Well, I've never seen one, but I wouldn't say it's not possible that they exist. Who is to say? I recall going into the little house and how it reminded me of Minnie Mouse's home in Disneyland, Florida. I went upstairs and lay on the bed. 'Ooh!' said the lady chuckling. 'Daniel O'Donnell is in my bed!'

Glenveagh Castle in Donegal is another magnificent location we used for a photo shoot and I would highly recommend a visit to the Glenveagh National Park. Although it's not far from where I live, I hadn't been there since I was a kid.

Yet another beautiful location that springs to mind from my photo shoots is the area near Cromleach Lodge Hotel in rural County Sligo. It has enchanting views of the unspoiled four-thousand-year-old Carrowkeel passage tomb cemetery, the second largest megalithic pile in Europe, as well as the lake and valley. It's a lovely place to relax and explore, with its five thousand archaeological sites as well as walking trails through fields and woodlands. I remember on that shoot how I had to climb over graves in my green wellies to get up to slippery steps at a monastery, reputed to be one of the oldest in Ireland. On the way back I discovered that it had been founded by the McDonaghs. I had probably been stepping on Mick's ancestors!

John Ryan, my record producer at Beechpark Studios, Rathcoole

While I love performing on stage, I have to admit that I've never been a big fan of the recording studio. I would rather have a sea of faces in front of me when I'm singing. Some performers spend months in the studio working on an album, but I have it down to a fine art. I'm in and out quicker than a thief in the night. I'm putting my coat on when I'm singing the last note and once the experts say, 'That's great!' I don't question them. I'm away like greyhounds after a hare.

That said, in recent times I've become a lot more laid back in that environment. That's probably to do with the fact that I enjoy working in Beechpark Studios, which are out in the countryside around Rathcoole, Co. Dublin. I love being in rural places looking out of the window over open spaces. My earlier recordings were done in city studios that had no windows and were often underground. I think I need the light.

I always feel very comfortable working with my producer John Ryan, who also used to be a member of my band. John can read me like a book at this stage of our relationship, so he knows how to bring out the best in me. One of my favourite recordings is the 2002 album, *Faith and Inspiration*. It was recorded in a Dublin venue called Temple Theatre – it used to be a church – and I just loved the sound of a magnificent sixty-piece orchestra behind me and the really inspiring choir that lifted me to another level. I felt I was floating on air. I could have gone straight up to heaven at that time, I was so exhilarated. I must have been very good in another life to deserve this, I thought.

Somebody who has played a very important role in my career recently, is the Irish singer/songwriter Marc Roberts. I've known Marc for many years, but it's only in recent times that we started songwriting together and I'm very proud of the songs we've penned. Hopefully, you enjoy them too.

Songwriting with Marc

In 1998, France was playing host to the soccer World Cup and I was in Paris to do a photo shoot for my LOVE SONGS album. Mick, being a rugby fan himself, had organised the picture session and the location totally oblivious of the fact that the City of Light was going to be swarming with soccer followers.

The night I arrived Mick couldn't understand why there were a million people blocking the streets of Paris. Later, he would confess to me, 'I was wondering why it was so hard to get hotel reservations.'

The next day as I was posing outside Les Deux Magots café, dressed in a white linen suit and with one of Mick's bloomin' red roses for company, there was a chorus of 'Danny Boy' resounding from every packed bar around the square. Scotland were playing in the big opening game and their Tartan Army of fans had spotted me. I'm a firm believer that it's always better to introduce yourself to people you haven't met and then they're in a better position to make up their minds about you as a person, so I strolled over to say hello to them. Before I knew it, those big fellas were thrusting mobile phones into my hand to talk to their loved ones back home in Scotland.

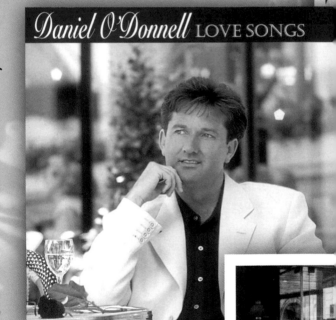

'Och, oh, I'm here with Daniel O'Donnell,' they'd say, before handing me the phone. I spoke to mothers, sisters, wives and mothers-in-law and it was great fun. They were good sports and I enjoyed the atmosphere. One fella in a kilt said to me, 'Och, I'll be all right now that my wife knows I'm with you. She won't be thinkin' I'm in the pub!'

I loved that Paris session. Although I don't go to France very much I love to hear the French accent and the people have a great air about them.

PARIS

Like the majority of people, I remember exactly where I was the moment I heard that Diana, Princess of Wales, had been in a car crash on 31 August 1997. I was staying with friends in America when the call came through from home. A woman called Eva, who lives in Derry, phoned to tell us.

'Have you the TV on? Diana has been in a car crash,' Eva said in a breathless tone. Father Michael Cannon, a friend from home who is a priest in the States, was with me at the time. It was about 11 o'clock where we were, and not long after the accident had happened. We turned on the TV and, sure enough, it was on the news. Bad news travels fast, as they say.

We watched the bulletins for a while and then there was the first shock: Diana's boyfriend Dodi Fayed was dead. I remember saying to Michael, 'This will finish Diana now.' I meant that, mentally, it would push her over the edge because I felt that she had had so much trauma in her life.

As we went to bed there was still no word on Diana's condition, apart from the fact that she'd been taken to hospital. The next morning Michael knocked on my door, came into the room and said, 'Diana didn't make it!' I went into a state of shock. I couldn't lift my head off the pillow. I couldn't even get up and say, 'What?' I was just stuck to the pillow.

My mother loved Princess Diana. She kept Diana scrapbooks with all kinds of cuttings – both stories and photographs – about the princess in it. I phoned my mother that morning to say how sorry I was that Diana was dead. When my mother answered the call she was crying.

I was surprised at the impact that Diana's death had on me because I wouldn't have said that she made a profound impression on me. I was very aware of her

LOCATIONS

Flowers for Princess Diana

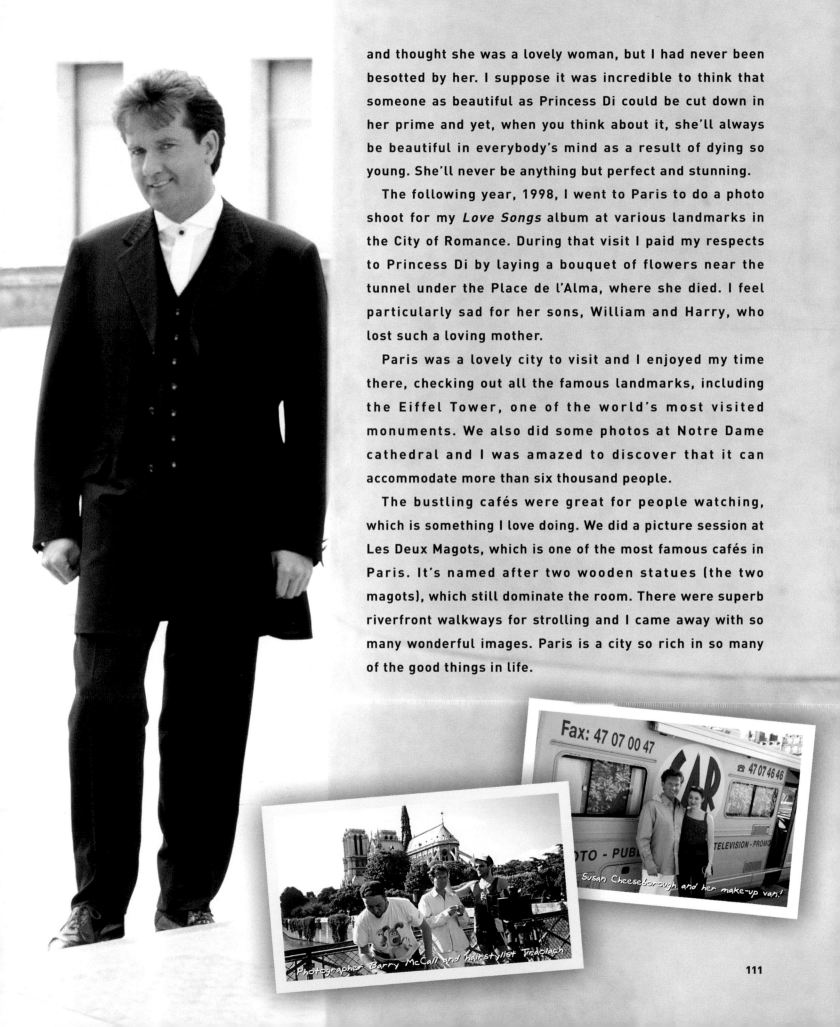

and thought she was a lovely woman, but I had never been besotted by her. I suppose it was incredible to think that someone as beautiful as Princess Di could be cut down in her prime and yet, when you think about it, she'll always be beautiful in everybody's mind as a result of dying so young. She'll never be anything but perfect and stunning.

The following year, 1998, I went to Paris to do a photo shoot for my *Love Songs* album at various landmarks in the City of Romance. During that visit I paid my respects to Princess Di by laying a bouquet of flowers near the tunnel under the Place de l'Alma, where she died. I feel particularly sad for her sons, William and Harry, who lost such a loving mother.

Paris was a lovely city to visit and I enjoyed my time there, checking out all the famous landmarks, including the Eiffel Tower, one of the world's most visited monuments. We also did some photos at Notre Dame cathedral and I was amazed to discover that it can accommodate more than six thousand people.

The bustling cafés were great for people watching, which is something I love doing. We did a picture session at Les Deux Magots, which is one of the most famous cafés in Paris. It's named after two wooden statues (the two magots), which still dominate the room. There were superb riverfront walkways for strolling and I came away with so many wonderful images. Paris is a city so rich in so many of the good things in life.

Fax: 47 07 00 47

47 07 46 46

Susan Cheeseborough and her make-up van!

Photographer Barry McCall and hair stylist Tredolach

PARK HOTEL

The Herbert Park hotel, set in the surroundings of leafy Ballsbridge on the south side of Dublin, has played a starring role in some of my photo shoots. And, weaving his magic, Mick even transformed its environs into Paris for a day, when we shot a TV commercial and promotional film there for the *Love Songs* album in 1999.

The Herbert Park is a very modern hotel and I have to be honest and say that I'm not a great lover of modern architecture. I feel those kinds of building are very clinical places and lacking in atmosphere. Mick, however, has another view, and he really liked the Herbert Park, having checked it out shortly after its opening. He was looking for somewhere special for me to show off the stylish stage suits I was using then, and he thought that hotel would make a fantastic location for the picture shoot.

The manager at the time was Michael McBride. He came from Donegal and knew me, so we had no problem getting in. The Herbert Park did provide a great backdrop and all the photographs turned out really well. I was very impressed.

My second visit to the Herbert Park turned into a comical affair for many reasons. We had done a cover for *Love Songs* outside the famous Les Deux Magots café in Paris, but long after we returned home the record company decided we needed a TV commercial and promo film for the album. Because of other commitments, it wasn't possible for me to make the trip back to the City of Light, so Mick had to

improvise. He remembered that the Herbert Park had a green roof at one side, just like Les Deux Magots, and there was also a traffic-free boulevard at the side of the hotel.

Mick then recreated a scene just like the photo we had taken in Paris for the cover of the album. He got a restaurant sign painted and put up, then added the same coffee table with the same cups and all the other details. To complete the picture he had a French Citroën car parked nearby. The day the scene was set up, the weather looked like Paris in the springtime. Mick makes plans and God smiles.

The next morning when we drew back the curtains, the Irish weather was having a laugh at us. A hurricane had been raging off Florida and had travelled across the Atlantic to spoil our shoot. It was the windiest and wettest day Dublin had experienced since meteorological records began! As it was the only day that I had free to do the shoot, Mick and the crew had to make the best of it. He sent out to a garden centre for a patio gazebo cover, which had to be strapped down because of the wind. But I still ended up getting blown to bits, even though all the trucks had been parked around me as shelter while I sang.

There were also some shots done on the balcony of a hotel suite, with me in a white bathrobe and gale-force winds coming around the corner! When the finished article appeared on TV you'd never have known that it wasn't shot in Paris on a nice day. Mind you, the two lovers who were featured looked as if they'd been carousing in the fountains – another soft day!

In 1999 I took a boat trip along the waterways of Ireland, from the north to the south of our country. It was for a video called *Peaceful Waters*, devised by my Mick, in which I was introduced to the experience of a tour by boat. The scenery was mesmerising, and there were interesting monuments, castles, stately homes and estates to visit, and lovely little pubs for leisurely lunches. It was like being on a holiday. I highly recommend such a journey. What a wonderful way to explore Ireland.

The *Peaceful Waters* video coincided with a concert I had planned for the Omagh Fund. It was a tribute to the people who lost their lives in that terrible bombing the previous year, and to the survivors who are coping with the aftermath of the shocking atrocity. I sang with the children there and it was a lovely, warm event.

With a theme of peace and reconciliation, *Peaceful Waters* opens with me straddling a deck on the water in Belleek, Co. Fermanagh. The significance was that I had one foot in Northern Ireland and one foot in the Republic. They say it rains a lot in Ireland and, if it does, that same rain falls on all of us. It doesn't differentiate between people and neither should we. Thanks to huge efforts of both the Irish

THE SENATOR MITCHELL "PEACE" BRIDGE

FINN-MAC-COOL

and British governments and, of course, our friends in America, the 150-year-old Ballyconnell Canal has been restored as the Shannon–Erne Waterway, or 'The Peace Canal', linking our two great rivers and all of the fantastic lakes.

You can peacefully cruise and meander from Belleek in County Donegal to Enniskillen, on to Carrick-on-Shannon and through to Limerick; from the Erne in the north, to where the Shannon meets the Atlantic Ocean in the south. There are some wonderful stories attached to landmarks along the route.

Around Lough Erne, there's a church with a tale that was the inspiration for a scene from the film *The Quiet Man*. In that movie the bishop visits a Protestant community with the intention of closing down the local church because of a decline in numbers. The Catholic priest helps to inflate the congregation by taking his people out for the visit and urging them to, 'Cheer like good Protestants!' A similar incident happened in one church on the waterway. The Protestant vicar enlisted the help of the local Catholic priest and asked if he could borrow some of his flock so that the numbers would be well up the day the bishop came. A friend in need is a friend indeed!

Ireland is steeped in history, myths and legends. For thousands of years many of the little islands along the waterway on the lakes were inhabited, some by hermits and monks who had travelled from across Europe to find peace, tranquillity and solitude. Many things hidden by time from those days are a complete mystery, like the ancient Janus figures on Boa island, or the early Christian figures on White Island, Lower Erne, which feature as a backdrop to some songs in the video.

I stopped off at the old town of Enniskillen, the county town of Fermanagh, where Oscar Wilde and Samuel Beckett went to school, as did Henry Francis, who wrote the wonderful song 'Abide With Me'. Along the journey I passed by some lovely estates and country houses. I also anchored not far from Florence Court House, which was donated to the National Trust by the son of the fifth Earl of Enniskillen. It has beautiful gardens and terrific views – a lovely place to visit.

There is also the old Crom Castle on the banks of Upper Lough Erne. It was built in the seventeenth century and survived two sieges before being burned down in 1764. Legend has it that Abraham Creighton buried all his gold near the castle before one of the battles and it's reputed to be still there. They say if anyone tries to dig it up a curse will fall on them. I wonder: is it worth the risk? At Castle Island I was reminded how WB Yeats wanted to acquire the castle so that he could have private time there with Maud Gonne, the great love of his life. It never came to pass.

Songs featured on the video include 'I Can See Clearly Now', 'The Way Old Friends Do', 'Cutting the Corn in Creeslough', 'An Irish Lullaby', 'I Believe', 'I Have a Dream', 'Beyond the Great Divide', 'When Hope Dawns at Sunrise', 'The Rose of Mooncoin', 'Even on Days When it Rained', 'Everything is Beautiful', 'Heaven Around Galway Bay' and 'Home to Donegal'. A lot of the songs were relative to the location or the situation.

Peaceful Waters is one of my favourite videos. I love the way it was constructed, the songs, my dialogue and the fact that it's informative. I was very relaxed presenting it and I adapted the script to suit myself, so it became more personal.

I think it's a very tranquil video and, even if you don't want to watch *me*, you'll certainly enjoy the scenery, which is just spectacular, and there's lovely haunting background music. Maybe someday I'll go back with Majella and we can enjoy the beauty of Ireland together at a leisurely pace on the waterways. And maybe we'll see you there too!

As for negotiating the boat through the waterways, well, I'll have you know that I did steer it myself. The hardest part was going into the locks and opening the gates, but I came through with flying colours.

RIVERSDALE BARGE HOLIDAYS
Tel. 078 - 44122
BALLINAMORE
COUNTY LEITRIM

CABINET OFFICE

Minister for the Cabinet Office
Chancellor of the Duchy of Lancaster

Michael J McDonagh
Cara Music Ltd
London

Dear Michael,

7 December 1999

PEACEFUL WATERS

Thank you for your letter of 25 November, enclosing Daniel's video.

After five years working on the Northern Ireland issue I am sad to be leaving so many friends and colleagues. I am sad to leave the beautiful countryside behind too. But I will be back sometime in the not too distant future, and your video will remind me of what I am missing!

Please pass on my thanks to Daniel.

Mo

MARJORIE MOWLAM

Walking through Shell Cottage on a grand estate in County Kildare, Ireland, I was filled with a sense of foreboding. Something about the place sent shivers down my spine and I was overcome with fear. I couldn't wait to get out of the place.

I was on the 1,100-acre Carton Demesne estate, a beautiful setting of trees and lawns surrounded by a five-mile-long wall near Maynooth, about a half-hour drive from Dublin. It was formerly the ancestral home of the Fitzgeralds, Earls of Kildare. One of the famous features of the demesne is Shell Cottage, which is decorated outside and inside with seashells and was built for Lady Emily Fitzgerald in the eighteenth century. At the time that I visited, Shell Cottage was home to Marianne Faithfull, the singing star who became famous in the sixties, although she wasn't in when we called.

Mick had secured permission from the owners to do some photographs at the location and we left a thank-you note for Marianne when we were leaving. I was filled with admiration for Marianne because she had the courage to live in that house. I didn't like it one bit. I thought it was spooky and if I was living in it I would be afraid every minute. I got a terrible cold feeling in it.

Carton House itself, though, was very majestic and really lovely. We did a Christmas card photo session there and got some lovely pictures. I'm told that the estate has now been developed as a major golf enterprise with a Colin Montgomerie course that's open to the public. As a golf fanatic, I might pay a return visit, but I'll steer clear of Shell Cottage!

There are so many stately homes like Carton House in Ireland and I often thought that I'd love to go back in time and see the lifestyle of the people who lived in them. I'm sure all they did was have a jolly time.

DEMESNE

Shell Cottage

Carton Demesne
A time honoured retreat-
for today

127

I think everyone has a summer they remember as one of the best times in their lives, and 1980 was mine. It was the period before I started college and I spent it in Dublin, working in the kitchen of the Central Hotel by day and having the time of my life by night.

Shortly after starting work, I struck up a friendship with two of the hotel staff, Margaret Coyle and Maura Cullinane, who, sadly, is no longer with us. We became inseparable. We laughed our way through that whole summer and we went dancing in Dublin every night to big Irish singing stars such as Big Tom, Philomena Begley and Susan McCann. One of my favourite venues from that period was the old style Ierne ballroom. I remember splashing out £70 – a fortune to me at the time – on an outfit to go dancing there, and I swanned around the place hoping that everyone would notice it! But people probably never gave me a second glance.

I get very nostalgic when I think about that time in my life and my nights at the Ierne, so imagine my feelings when I returned there in 1999 to shoot a video for my single, 'A Christmas Kiss', with the British TV character Mrs Merton (Caroline Aherne) making a guest appearance. It reminded me of how far I had travelled in my life, thanks to singing and the support of people who enjoy what I do.

One of my best TV appearances in the UK was on *The Mrs Merton Show*, so I was delighted when Caroline agreed to do the video. She plays a battleaxe office manager and I'm the post boy. But, when she spots me looking like a rock hunk in a band at the office party, Mrs Merton is overcome with passion and ploughs through the dancers with mistletoe to plant a big kiss on my lips!

May Lynch & Mrs Merton

Daniel O'Donnell
A CHRISTMAS Kiss

Fans Mr and Mrs Kelly drop in to meet Caroline and me

Yet another studio session...

This horse is going to make me sneeze!

AND SPICY

It's almost a sin to enjoy the beautiful sights that Glenveagh Castle in County Donegal has to offer. As I mentioned earlier, I did a photo shoot there and, during that visit, I took the opportunity to look into the history of the estate. It was then I learned the awful truth that it was established in 1861 by a man called John Adair, who built it up by buying several smallholdings. He then became notorious in Ireland when he evicted his 244 tenants and cleared the land so that his views of the breath-taking landscape wouldn't be hindered.

Adair built Glenveagh Castle about 1870, but died in 1885. His wife survived him until 1921, but, unlike her husband, she is remembered as a kind and generous person. From 1937 until 1983, Glenveagh was the summer residence of Henry McIlhenny, a wealthy Philadelphian art collector, who was of Donegal ancestry and a member of the famous McIlhenny Tabasco Sauce family. I believe McIlhenny, who was once described as 'the only person in Philadelphia with glamour', hosted many wonderful parties at Glenveagh when it was his summer residence.

His guests included such luminaries as Greta Garbo, Noël Coward and the celebrated violinist Yehudi Menuhin. There's a story told that local fiddlers used to provide entertainment for the guests and Yehudi joined them one time. Some time later, one of the fiddlers said to McIlhenny, 'Is that Hughie McMenamin boy ever coming back? He was a fair good fiddler.'

Although he spent only three months there every year, Henry McIlhenny invested huge sums improving and enlarging the garden. A generous man, in 1983 he gave the castle and its gardens to the Irish nation to form the centrepiece of a 28,000-acre national park. Today it's a wonderful place to visit, despite the story behind its origins. The setting includes woodlands, herds of red deer, alpine gardens and a sylvan lake, as well as the impressive view of Errigal Mountain. I loved the tour of the castle.

137

ROCK

DANIEL

Rock'n'roll has always been a popular feature of my live show, but I never realised how much my audience loved those songs from the fifties and sixties till a record label called Demon approached us to release them on an album. Just as my success in America has come as a surprise to me, sales of the rock'n'roll albums went far beyond anything I ever expected and their performance in the charts has been astonishing.

My first release was called DANIEL IN BLUE JEANS, a compilation of favourite rock'n'roll love songs. It comprised 'Singing the Blues', 'Teenager in Love', 'Never Be Anyone Else But You', 'Love Me Tender', 'Halfway To Paradise', 'Blueberry Hill', 'Bye Bye Love', 'It Doesn't Matter Anymore', 'Travelling Light', 'A Fool Such As I', 'Roses Are Red', 'Save the Last Dance for Me', 'Donna', 'Send Me the Pillow That You Dream On', 'Wooden Heart', 'Young Love', 'Twelfth of Never',

'Honey', 'Green Green Grass of Home' and 'Sealed with a Kiss'. Some of them were a part of my show and some were new, but they were all very well received by the fans, judging by the response that I got from the people I met along the way.

When my second collection, THE JUKEBOX YEARS, was released, it went straight up to Number 3 in the British charts. I could hardly believe it. That album featured such highlights as 'Hello, Mary Lou', 'Oh Boy', 'Come On Over to My Place', 'Daydream Believer', 'Sweet Caroline', 'Is This the Way to Amarillo' and a Mary Duff duet, 'Walk Right Back'. It had always been my intention to record the rock'n'roll section of my show. They are great songs to perform, a lot of fun and a very upbeat experience for both me and, I hope, the audience.

Receiving my platinum disc from David Smith (Rosette) and Michael Neidus (Demon)

As I write, I am now making plans to do a rock'n'roll tour, in addition to the gospel shows, the Christmas/gospel concerts and my regular stage performance.

I was skipping down the stairs of Dublin's Temple Theatre when I met the manager of the venue on his way up.

'How are you, Daniel?' he greeted me. 'It's hard auld going!'

He was implying that my job recording a video that day was stressful and wearing. And that sentiment couldn't have been further from the thoughts that were going through my mind at the time. I was shooting a video for my song, 'The Way Dreams Are', in the Temple Theatre, and I was reflecting on how amazing it was to think that this is what I do for a living. I was thrilled to be there doing the video and was enjoying every moment of it. I was obviously used to the process by then. When I took a step back and saw all the crew setting up the venue for MY big shoot, I mentally acknowledged my good fortune.

THE WAY DREAMS ARE was a modern video that pretended that the Temple Theatre was a big recording session, just like one the Beatles might have done at the famous Abbey Road studios in London. I loved the way it turned out. I've always enjoyed the atmosphere of the Temple Theatre, a venue where Whitney Houston, Bobby Brown and even Puff Daddy have performed live when they were in town for one of the big MTV Europe Awards. So I guess if it's good enough for Puff Daddy then it's surely good enough for me.

It's also the venue where, as I have already mentioned, I recorded the album I regard as my masterpiece – the FAITH AND INSPIRATION collection – backed by a sixty-piece orchestra and choir.

There are guys called critics and, if I had paid any attention to what a lot of them wrote and said about me during my time as a singer, I would have packed in my career long ago. But they were never going to influence me.

The only people I ever cared about were the audience and the fans. Once I knew that people really enjoyed what I had to offer, that was the only reaction that mattered to me. You have to believe in what you're doing and, irrespective of what anyone says to you or what anybody writes about you, you have to really try not to let it affect you.

As a teenager, I was a huge fan of an Irish singing star called Philomena Begley. One day I called at her home looking for advice. 'Philomena,' I said, 'I want to become a singer.'

She was up to her elbows in flour baking bread at that moment. Philomena stopped what she was doing and, after a long pause, said, 'Daniel, I really think you should stick to the books.'

It wasn't what I wanted to hear, but, with hindsight, I realise Philomena was telling me how hard it is to become successful in show business. But I had tunnel vision. There was only one route I was ever going to take in life and that was on to a stage. My advice to everyone is to go for your dream. If you don't achieve it, at least you'll never die wondering. Find a job you love and you'll never work a day in your life.

In 1992, I did an album called *Follow Your Dream* and we did a photo shoot for the cover in Cardiff. I recall that there were a lot of clothes for that session, but, as we were shooting in a park on a cold day, I borrowed Mick's pink sweater. When the pictures were selected for the album cover, the one of me in Mick's cosy sweater was selected. I never did pay him for the hire of it!

Presented by
DANIEL O'DONNELL
to
BELCRUIT NATIONAL SCHOOL
18th April 1990
"FOLLOW YOUR DREAM, I DID"

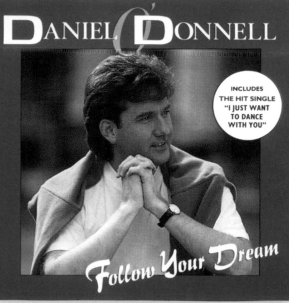

DANIEL O'DONNELL

INCLUDES THE HIT SINGLE "I JUST WANT TO DANCE WITH YOU"

Follow Your Dream

The little village church in Kincasslagh is dear to my heart for many reasons. It was in there that I married Majella in November, 2002. And it's the church where I had my first experience of singing in public, as a member of the choir when I was a child. I've always loved singing in the chapel, whether it was during Mass or for weddings.

My faith is a very important part of my life and I realised that after I moved away from home. When I lived in my local community I attended Mass every Sunday with the rest of my family. Some people do it for appearances' sake when they're at home, but I found when I went on the road that I needed that little bit of spirituality. It gives meaning to my life. It doesn't make me any better or worse than anybody else. It just makes me feel good.

I also love the fact that I've been given the opportunity to record the albums of faith and inspiration. They are special to me on a personal level because of my faith in God. I have also had the privilege of personally writing two hymns, which came to me when I was on a pilgrimage to Medjugorje, a small mountain village in Bosnia, where the Virgin Mary is said to have appeared to six young visionaries in June 1981, and continued to do so to this day. The words came into my mind and I wrote 'Sweet Queen of Peace' and 'When Darkness Falls', both of which I have now recorded. Everybody says you are 'invited' to Medjugorje for a reason. And I believe that is the reason I felt compelled to go there. My ambition is to go back and sing those two hymns in the church at Medjugorje.

G I V E   A   L I

In 1998 I went to Romania to make a video for my charity single, 'Give a Little Love'. While there I witnessed at first hand the terrible legacy of the dictator Nicolae Ceauşescu: hundreds of children were enduring a life of hell in a cold, rat-infested building with no heat, no stimulation and no love. I saw terrible sights of children suffering from physical deformities because of their ill treatment.

I will never forget the stench that greeted me when I walked through the door of that institution. And it was then I resolved to use my celebrity to help those pitiful young people. Two women from home, Eileen Oglesby and Sheila Mulholland, had asked for my support and I decided to do the single to raise money. At the time, I had no intention of getting involved with the work of the charity. But I was so affected by what I experienced on my visit and I made such a strong connection with the children that I knew I would never be able to walk away from it. It was my opportunity to help make a difference in life. And I feel it's a privilege that that honour came to me.

When I came home, I started talking about the Romanian charity and the plight of the orphans at my shows, and I appealed to my audiences for financial donations to help out. With the money that was raised by all the people who answered my call, we have been able to build houses, buy a farm and integrate young people back into the community where some of them are working in local industry. Many of them now have a good quality of life, thanks to the generosity and thoughtfulness of the fans and people in general who acted on my appeals.

Our work goes on in Romania. It's a daunting task as there are still many more children to be rescued. But to put a smile on the face of even one young person makes it all worthwhile.

The Romanian Challenge Appeal

1. Máire Rua cartoon   2. Left to right: John Francis, Siobhan, James, Fiona, Sharon, Michael, PJ, Patricia myself and Majella   3. At the alter, just after we arrived   4. With Sean Reilly (my manager), his wife Olive and daughter Pamela   5. All my immediate family members!   6. Majella's mum and dad Marion and Thomas Roche   7. With Sean Reilly, my manager   8. PJ Sweeney (best man) Michael McLennan (groom's man), James O'Donnell (groom's man), and John Francis Doogan (groom's man)   9. With my new wife and my mother   10. This was taken at home before I left for the church (left to right) brother James, sister Kathleen, me, mother and John my brother   11. Fiona and Patricia Doogan (my two nieces), Siobhan McLennan (Majella's daughter) and Sharon Sweeney (PJ Sweeneys daughter and my God child)

153

154

1. Can I have this dance for the rest of my life?   2. Cutting the cake   3. At the top table   4. Leaving church on the way to Letterkenny   5. Majella with her daughter Siobhan and my nieces Patricia and Fiona   6. A moment for the media cameras!   7. Kissing for the media cameras!   8. Singing "When I Found You" with Marc Roberts   9. As we were pronounced man and wife

that on my fortieth I would do nothing. But when it came around – far too quickly for my liking! – I was involved with the Romanian charity and it provided the perfect opportunity to do a fundraising event. So, on 12 December 2001, I was joined by 1,200 people in the ballroom of Birmingham's Hilton Hotel for my birthday party. It raised in excess of £50,000 sterling for our work in Romania.

That night at the Hilton I introduced my girlfriend, Majella, to the world. At Christmas we became engaged and our wedding took place the following November. It was a fairytale affair for us, but I'm sure everyone feels the same about their own wedding. In particular, the ceremony in the little church of Kincasslagh, where I sang in the choir as a child, was just beautiful. To us, that was the most important aspect of our wedding day.

I loved the fact that so many of the fans came along to the church that day to give us their love and best wishes. And we felt like royalty as the people of Donegal braved the rain and held a vigil to see us on the route to the hotel reception in Letterkenny. There were bonfires lit along the roads and at one location a lone piper serenaded us. When we reached the hotel it was like the Oscars ceremony, with screams and cheers from the crowd outside. It's a wonderful memory.

So how have I taken to married life? Well, I can honestly tell you that I have never been happier. My life is now more fulfilled as a result of sharing it with a wonderful person like Majella. It's lovely to have someone to make plans with, and we enjoy our time together.

AT HOME

If you asked me to name the two most important requirements for my dream home, I would answer: Majella and Donegal. And I am now a lucky man to have both in my life. My home is very much centred on Majella's presence there. When I walk through the door and she's not there, it's just a house; I feel there is something missing. It's such a lovely feeling when she's around.

I moved from house to house throughout my career. The environs of Dublin were my base for a time. In particular, I bought, renovated and decorated a lovely residence in the countryside at Rathcoole, Co. Dublin. That became my hobby for a time and I had a lot of fun working on it. The alterations and renovations took nine months to finish. I had a little sitting room off the master bedroom because I'd got used to that layout from staying in hotels. There was a king-size bed with a canopy, and it had a balcony with spectacular views of Dublin Bay in the distance. At night the twinkling lights of the city were just lovely and I never drew the curtains.

Outside, there was a beautiful garden with a pond. It was sheer luxury, but it didn't feel like home. When I sold it, I moved back to Donegal, turned our family cottage into a dormer bungalow and incorporated my own living area.

Since Majella came into my life we have found a lovely home by the sea at Cruit, not far from my family residence. We have had it redesigned and, as I write, it's being transformed into our dream place. It has turned out to be a much bigger house than we initially envisaged and it's more than we need, but I look upon it as a gift to us and I hope that's not selfish. I'm not a very extravagant person by nature. I don't buy a new car every year; at the moment I'm driving a BMW that's five years old and it recently failed the National Car Test, so I'll have to change it.

One of my passions, though, is houses. I absolutely love going to view show houses when I'm on holidays. Majella and I did that in Florida and ended up buying a lovely house, which we've since sold. The main feature of our new home in Cruit is a big entrance hall with a grand staircase. It's like something out of *Gone with the Wind*. All we need is a good breeze – and we get plenty of those in Donegal too!

It's like living on a boat because the house is sitting on the shore of the Atlantic Ocean. We look out of our windows at views of the sea with Errigal Mountain framed in the distance. From another angle, we can gaze upon Arranmore Island. Sunrise and sunset over the sea are absolutely beautiful times of the day in this setting. There's a deck below the house and in the summertime we can talk to the fishermen in their boats on the water as they pass by.

It's a wonder I ever leave that house at all! It just goes to show how much I still love the stage.

The grand piano was a first anniversary present from Majella

Well, here we are at the end of the journey up to now, and I hope you have enjoyed it. As you have seen, I've been fortunate to have enjoyed so many interesting and personally rewarding experiences because of you, the fans, and maybe you will explore some of the places I've visited. I hope that this look behind the scenes in my world has added to your enjoyment of who I am as a person, and that it has given you an insight into where I come from and what I do. Thank you for being there with me through so much of it. And, hopefully, our journey together will continue long into the future.

Daniel